BLESSINGS, PRAYERS, & HEART SONGS

BLESSINGS, PRAYERS, & HEART SONGS

CHARLENE QUINT

Deep River BOOKS

Published by
Deep River Books
Sisters, Oregon
www.deepriverbooks.com

ISBN-13: 9781940269276
ISBN-10: 194026927X

Library of Congress: 2014915694
Printed in the USA

Design by Robin Black, www.InspirioDesign.com

For Donny, Christy, and Marty:
You are the joy of my life. My greatest blessing is God choosing me to be your mom.

With love to my sister and friend, Kathy, and her family: Ron, Nicholas, and Sean.

To dear friends who have been the hands and feet of Jesus, seen the good in me and overlooked my many faults, rejoiced in life's celebrations, supported me during the valleys, and inspired me to write these blessings. You have blessed me beyond measure, and it is a privilege to be called your friend. In no particular order: Regina, Giel, Tommy, Christiane, Thomas, Addison, Sherry, Katie, Julie, Kira, Gino, Sue, Miriam, Kelly, Lisa, Beth, Gordon, Tatiana, Dan, Tiana, Jordan, Hutha, Jean, Jerry, Tisha, Chris, Rosemary, Peggy, Terry, Dana, John R., Betty, Monica, Christian, Kai, Leslie, Johnny Mac, Orley, Tommy D., Debbie, Kay, John K., Paula, Madison, Jordan A., Emmett, Anne, Cynthia, and John the Dog.

To the wonderful teachers, doctors, nurses, pastors, and firemen who have blessed all those who are fortunate enough to know them with their dedication, professionalism, and compassion: Peggy Usher, Larry Powell, Victoria Amesbury MD, the nurses at Northwestern Hospice, the Lake Forest fire department, Garth Warren, Mike Woodruff, Bob Thomas, Chris Stephens.

In honor of the United States military.
A grateful nation has been blessed beyond measure by your courage and commitment.

In memory of my parents, Richard and Jean Quint.
Theirs is a love story for the ages. By their example of humble, thankful, and generous spirits, they showed us how to live, and they even showed us how to die.

To those who, like me, have experienced the trauma of living with a narcissistic or have known the pain of domestic abuse—whether physical, emotional, verbal, sexual, financial, or spiritual— know that you are a Child of the King and that our heavenly Father wants us to live an abundant life filled with His Presence and joy, not a life of abuse. A portion of the profits of this book will be donated to charities that support women and children who are recovering from domestic abuse.

CONTENTS

❧

INTRODUCTION

*"Kindness is the language which the deaf can hear
and the blind can see."*
Mark Twain

How the human soul longs for encouragement, a gracious word, kindness that will lift our hearts and inspire us! Again and again, we reread those crumpled letters with words that give wings to our dreams and stream sunlight on the storms of life. We save those voice mail messages just to replay the sound of a gentle voice saying, "I love you. I believe in you. You can do it." How many of us have been spurred on to do great things that we didn't even know we could do by the encouragement of just one person who believed in us? And how many troubled souls have shriveled up, fallen into depression, and even taken their own lives because of constant criticism?

Words are powerful things. God knows that we need kind words for our spirits to flourish. He made us this way! But he also knows that the tongue can be a difficult thing to tame. When our days are more like survival in the jungle than a lovely walk with Jesus in the garden, our tongues can recite beautiful verses one minute and spit out ugly curses the next (James 3:3–10).

That's why God implores us with the love of a dad for his children to "not let any wholesome talk come out of [our] mouths, but only what is helpful for building others up according to their needs, that it may benefit those who listen." He wants us to "Get rid of all bitterness, rage and anger, brawling and slander, along with every form of malice." Instead, he urges us to "Be kind and compassionate to one another, forgiving each other, just as in Christ God forgave you" so that our conversations are "filled with grace" (Ephesians 4:29, 31, 32; Colossians 4:6).

In other words, every word we speak should be a blessing to others. I like to think that each word is a gift especially picked for the recipient, tucked with tissues of loveliness inside a beautiful silver box of graciousness and wrapped with a golden bow of love. Who would not be thrilled to get that as a present! And what happens when we speak with grace and encourage others? Unsurprisingly, the Holy Spirit encourages us as well, and the blessing comes back to us. That's just how God works.

I need constant reminders of this truth. And so, throughout my house and office, I have interspersed tiny gift boxes—some silver or porcelain, others paper or crystal, all beautiful and all with a bow on top—as daily remembrances that my words need to be "gifts of grace" to those who receive them. On the hall table outside my bedroom, I keep a veritable collection of lovely boxes so that every morning as I pass by them to start my day, I can ask the Holy Spirit to use my words that day to be a blessing to others. And every evening before I tuck the children into bed and kiss good night the family I love, I am reminded that these precious ones are God's gifts to me and that they especially need to hear, as the last voice of their day, God's grace from the words of my mouth.

Our words can give life. Our words can tell others that we believe in them, even more than they believe in themselves. Our words can be the magic dust that, when sprinkled on another soul, causes them to sparkle and propels them on to achieve the great things God has uniquely designed and equipped them to do. Our words can be the angelshine that heals the wings of an angel who has forgotten how to fly. Our words can be the catalyst that inspires, blesses, and encourages the hearts of those people God has intentionally placed in our lives to be all that God has planned for them to be. And by reaching out with kindness to others, we ourselves are inspired and blessed and encouraged.

Sadly, our words can also be a bitter knife that deeply wounds the heart of another soul whom God loves, causing it to never fully achieve the thriving life that our heavenly Father so desires for us. And in so doing—in damaging others—we damage ourselves as well.

Our calling as followers of Christ is to be Jesus with skin on. The only hands and feet God has here on earth are ours. The only eyes and ears God has here on earth are ours. The only mouth God has here on earth is ours.

Lord, may we submit our hearts to you so that our words are blessings, prayers, and gifts of grace.

HISTORY OF BLESSINGS

❧

A blessing is one of life's precious gifts. It is an invoking of God's favor upon a cherished person or nation or place or thing. It is a prayer requesting that our heavenly Father grant favor, open the doors of heaven, allow his kingdom to reign here on earth, and shower us with his divine mercies of love and prosperity and other good things. When we bless someone, when we say "May you be blessed," we may do the asking, but it is God, the source of all good gifts, who grants the blessing.

In addition to an action, a blessing is also a noun, meaning a wonderful, undeserved gift from Above. Properly considered, all the good things in our lives are gifts from Above. Whether good parents, a wonderful spouse, children, a nice home, a good job, living in a free nation—even our health, intelligence, prosperity, and the ability to earn a good living—all that we have are blessings from the Lord. When we come to the full realization that literally all good things in our lives are gifts from God, we are humbled and thankful. And that is when God can truly come into our hearts and mold us into the people he designed us to be—each one of us a person with a remarkable family resemblance to our heavenly Father above.

The tradition of bestowing a blessing dates back to ancient times. In Scripture, there are numerous mentions of blessings bestowed by God upon his leaders and upon the nation of Israel, as well as blessings requested by a leader upon his people, by a father upon his children, by a family upon a bride, and by Jesus upon his followers.

When God called Abraham to follow him and go to a new land, his calling also brought forth a blessing upon Abraham: "I will make you into a great nation and I will bless you; I will make your name great and you will be a blessing. I will bless those who bless you, and whoever curses you I will curse; and all peoples of the earth will be blessed through you" (Genesis 12: 2–3). Some years later, God again spoke with Abraham and blessed him and his wife, Sarah:

As for me, this is my covenant with you: You will be a father of many nations . . . I will make you very fruitful; I will make nations of you, and kings will come from you. I will establish my covenant as an everlasting covenant between me and you and your descendants after you for the generations to come, to be your God and the God of your descendants after you . . . I will bless [Sarah] and will surely give you a son by her. I will bless her so that she will be the mother of nations; kings of peoples will come from her. (Genesis 17: 4–7, 16)

Indeed, God did bless Abraham and his descendants—the Israelites and today's Jewish people—through whom blessings have flowed to countless others throughout the world.

In the Scriptures, more than mere lovely words, blessings spoken to a favored one by a person whose heart followed after the great Jehovah were truly powerful. God honored the requests of those who honored him and lived lives in obedience to him. The blessings bestowed upon a loved one came to fruition not only in his or her life, but also carried through to future generations.

Blessings were given in anticipation of marriage. As Rebekah left her family to join Abraham's family and marry Isaac, she and her family knew that the marriage was destined by God. Before her journey, her family gave the bride their blessing: "Our sister, may you increase to thousands upon thousands; may your offspring possess the gates of their enemies" (Genesis 24:60). Years later, as Isaac and Rebekah's son Jacob journeyed to find and marry his own wife, Isaac blessed him with these words:

May God Almighty bless you and make you fruitful and increase your numbers until you become a community of peoples. May he give you and your descendants the blessing given to Abraham, so that you may take possession of the land where you now live as an alien, the land God gave to Abraham. (Genesis 28:3–4)

Blessings were bestowed by a father upon his children. The blessing that an aging father gave to his sons was so important that Esau was heartbroken and wept bitterly when he learned that his father Isaac, old and blind at the time, had been deceived into giving a blessing intended for Esau, as the eldest son, to Esau's younger brother, Jacob. Because of this blessing, it was Jacob, not Esau, who became one of the founding fathers of the Israelites and who was in the ancestral line of Jesus.

Jacob had twelve sons, which became the twelve tribes of Israel, and he blessed each one of them before he died. (Admittedly, it is difficult to characterize some of these as "blessings," as Jacob withdrew his favor from some of his sons who had committed egregious wrongs.) Because Jacob withdrew his blessing from his firstborn son, Reuben, and gave the blessing of rulership and victory over his enemies to Judah, it was through Judah's lineage that Jesus was born.

Jacob also gave a special blessing to Joseph, who had been sold into slavery in Egypt by his brothers and who saved his entire family from a famine that swept through their land when he became a leader in Egypt, second only to Pharaoh. Jacob's blessing upon Joseph included Joseph's sons, Ephraim and Manasseh:

> May God before whom my fathers Abraham and Isaac walked, the God who has been my shepherd all my life to this day, the Angel who has delivered me from all harm—may he bless these boys. May they be called by my name and the names of my fathers Abraham and Isaac, and may they greatly increase upon the earth. (Genesis 48:15–16)

Foretelling the blessings over Jewish boys that are spoken even to this day, Jacob said of his grandchildren, "In your name will Israel pronounce this blessing: 'May God make you like Ephraim and Manasseh'" (Genesis 48:20).

Blessings were also given upon the people of the nation of Israel. One of the most well-known blessings is known as the Priestly Blessing. The Lord instructed Moses to tell his brother Aaron, a priest, to bless the people with this blessing:

> The Lord bless you and keep you; the Lord make his face shine upon you and be gracious unto you; the Lord turn his face towards you and give you peace. (Numbers 6:24–26)

What a wonderful thought that the Maker of the Universe wants to shower us with his favor, keep us safe in his loving arms, smile at us and illuminate us, give us undeserved grace, and grant us peace to calm our hearts in a troubled world because we know that our trust lies in him!

Blessings were bestowed upon wives and mothers. One of my favorite passages is Proverbs 31, in which a woman of noble character is described. She is a woman who conducts business, cares for her household and family, helps the needy, and is prepared for the future. She is "clothed with strength and dignity" and "speaks with wisdom" (Proverbs 31: 25, 26). Her husband is a leader in the community; he trusts her and praises her. Her children and her husband recognize the gift they have in this wonderful woman, and they bless her: "Many women do noble things, but you surpass them all" (Proverbs 31:29). Perhaps this is the biblical version of today's joyful outburst of, "Mommy, you're the best mommy in the whole wide world!"

In Jesus's Sermon on the Mount, Jesus bestows blessings on those followers who have attitudes that are favored of God. Unlike the blessings in the Old Testament, which often went through family lineage, Jesus assures us that God will bless all who humbly seek him. In one of these blessings, which have come to be known as the Beatitudes, Jesus promises: "Blessed are the pure in heart, for they will see God." I'm not sure if there can be any greater blessing than that.

> Blessed are the poor in spirit,
>   for theirs is the kingdom of heaven.
> Blessed are those who mourn,
>   for they will be comforted.
> Blessed are the meek,
>   for they will inherit the earth.
> Blessed are those who hunger and thirst for righteousness,
>   for they will be filled.
> Blessed are the merciful,
>   for they will be shown mercy.
> Blessed are the pure in heart,
>   for they will see God.
> Blessed are the peacemakers,
>   for they will be called children of God.
> Blessed are those who are persecuted because of righteousness,
>   for theirs is the kingdom of heaven.

> Blessed are you when people insult you, persecute you and falsely say all kinds of evil against you because of me. Rejoice and be glad, because great is your reward in heaven, for in the same way they persecuted the prophets who were before you. (Matthew 5:3–12)

Today, in some observant Jewish homes, blessings are still given during a Friday evening Shabbat dinner. As foretold by Jacob, the father or the parents ask for a blessing upon the boys with these words: "May you be like Ephraim and Manasseh." A blessing for the girls is requested with "May you be like Sarah, Rebekah, Rachel, and Leah." The children are then blessed with the Priestly Blessing. In a beautiful act of love, the husband reads Proverbs 31 and speaks words of blessing and praise over his wife. Blessings are asked upon the dinner, and thankful praise is given to God.

However, for most families, the ancient tradition of bestowing a blessing, of asking for God's favor upon a son or daughter or wife, has all but been lost in modern times. Bestowing a blessing on loved ones or upon special occasions has also gone the way of the dinosaur.

This book was written to remind us of the wonderful gift we are able to give when we ask the Lord's blessing upon the special people we cherish as we live in community with one another and celebrate the special occasions and rites of passage in our lives and in the lives of those around us. As were the blessings of the ancient ones, blessings are much more than nice words—they are fervent prayers requesting God's favor. And as he did for those who have gone before us, God honors the earnest requests of his people who seek him and are obedient.

Whether we are entering into marriage, welcoming a new baby into the world, moving into a new home, remembering a birthday, celebrating an anniversary, recognizing a graduation, requesting safety for those in the armed services, or saying good-bye to a loved one who has been called home to the Lord, the most wonderful gift we could ever give or receive is that the Lord himself would be in the midst of the special events in our lives and in the lives of those whom we care about. And whether those whom we care about are family members, friends, teachers, physicians, or others who have blessed us by being in our lives, we treasure those we treasure, we cherish those we cherish, and we love those we love when we ask the Lord to rain his blessings upon them.

WEDDINGS, ANNIVERSARIES, AND LOVE

❧

Marriage was designed by God to be the most intimate and sacred of relationships. God designed marriage to be a microcosm of heaven: full of mutual love, kindness, and acceptance. In Ephesians 5, Paul tells husbands that they must love their wives no less than in the way Christ loved each of us, even to the point of sacrificing their lives. And he tells wives to respect their husbands. Just as we love because Christ first loved us, husbands are called to be the leaders in showing love first, and when a wife feels loved and safe and secure, she blossoms and responds with love and respect. This magical formula—of a husband loving his wife just as Jesus loves her, and a wife responding in love—is God's perfect design for us to reach our full potential and bloom into all he has designed us to be. Paul goes on to say that both husbands and wives should in humbleness submit to each other out of their love for Christ. There is no room in marriage for selfishness or pride, both of which are enemies of love. Those are tall orders. But that is how God wired us, and if we follow these instructions, marriage can be a little bit of heaven on earth.

I wrote my first blessing over ten years ago when I was invited to two weddings for four dear friends—Giel and Regina and Tom and Christiane. I took a look at their wedding registries and felt uninspired by the seemingly endless list of towels, dinnerware, and designer kitchen appliances. I knew that both couples would be quite successful in their careers and would be able to purchase as many designer toasters as they could ever want. I wanted to give them something meaningful and memorable—something that would not be forgotten in the pile of Crate and Barrel boxes and tissue paper. Something that, over the course of the next fifty years, they could look at and smile and say, "Charlene gave us that."

What I really wanted to give them was something they, and every married couple, need—a happy, loving, fulfilling marriage. But of course, that was not mine to give. That is God's to give. So, after some contemplation, I asked the Lord to give them just that. I sat down in the study late one evening, and with a Bible in my left hand and a pen in my right, I wrote a blessing asking the Lord to bless them with all the wonderful things God had designed for them. I asked God to bless them with love, joy, peace, patience, kindness, goodness, faithfulness, righteousness, wisdom, good health, prosperity, the Lord's guidance, laughter, family, friends, children, and grandchildren. I framed the blessing and gave it to them (in addition to that designer toaster). It remains on their bedroom dresser to this day. And thus began the first of many blessings.

OUR WEDDING PRAYER

May we Love,
Even when the other is unlovely.
May we multiply each other's Joys
And divide each other's Sorrows.

May our Home be a haven of Peace
In the midst of the storms of life.
May we be Patient and Understanding,
Especially when the other needs it most.

May Kindness be imprinted
Upon all our words and deeds.
May Goodness and Righteousness be our mark,
Even when it is unpopular.

May Wisdom be a light unto our way
And a lamp to guide our path.
May we Delight in our Beloved
And be forever captivated by the Love of our youth.

May Self-Restraint and Faithfulness be our guides
In the midst of life's temptations.
May Health and Prosperity follow us
Wherever we may go.

May Laughter and Friends and Family
Always fill our home.
May Forgiveness and Graciousness be freely given
And humbly accepted.

May we live to see our Children's Children,
And may they rise up and call us Blessed.
May we seek the Lord's guidance in all that we do
And in all that we say.

May we be a reflection of God's Love,
And may we dwell in God's Grace and under the Shelter of His Wings
As long as we both shall live.

LOVE EXTRAVAGANTLY

Let us outdo each other in kindness.
Let our hearts be forever thankful for the gift from God
That we have in each other.
Let us cherish our moments together and waste not one.

Let us each treasure the other as one who is
Wondrously and wonderfully made.
Let us be a blessing overflowing to one another.
Let us encourage each other so that our souls can soar.

Let us inspire each other to be better than we ever thought possible.
Let us be better together than apart.
Let us lead each other closer to God as daily we become more like him.
Let us protect the hearts we have entrusted to each other.
Let us be gracious, abiding securely in each other's unending grace.

Let us laugh in the rain, dance in the sun,
And cling closely in the storms.
Let our tango be playful and passionate, sweet and tender,
Gentle and kind, faithful and true.
Let us come back to each other,
To our safe place in the eye of the storm.

Let us give rather than take, seek to serve rather than be served,
Bring joy rather than sorrow, and seek peace rather than disharmony.
Let us give of ourselves freely and completely, with nothing held back.

And when have come to the end of our days that God has ordained,
Let us know that we have loved—and have been loved—extravagantly.

OUR LOVE

We are always good.

I love you, and I know you love me.

I want to spend life with you: I know you want to spend life with me.

If we happen to drift, as relationships are wont to do,
please bring us back together, don't walk away.

We are better together than apart.

Our love is kind and tender.

Our love always assumes the best in each other.

Our love always assumes the other has good intentions,
even if words or actions do not come out as intended.

Our love is patient.

Our love doesn't keep score.

It is more important for us to be in a good relationship
than to be right or to win.

Our love is not easily offended.

Our love forgives easily (even when not asked to).

Our love exercises self-control.

Our love sees the positive in any circumstance.

Our love sees humor in situations.

Our love seeks peace.

Our love is joyful.

Our love gives and affirms and encourages.

Our love seeks to be the love of God to one another.

A FIFTIETH ANNIVERSARY CELEBRATION

Fifty years of waking each morning
To the same lovely face.
At first smooth and fresh,
Filled with the hope and promise of youthful love.
And now even more beautifully adorned
With lines and a touch of gray,
Marking years of smiles, the wisdom of experience,
And promises fulfilled.

Fifty years of watching winter turn to spring,
Of new buds and unfolding flowers.
Fifty years of watching spring turn to summer,
Of warm July days, fireflies at night, and lazy summer evenings.
Fifty years of watching summer turn to autumn,
Of falling leaves, bountiful harvests, and hearts filled with thanksgiving.
Fifty years of watching autumn turn to winter,
Of sharing Christmas . . . of sharing each other.

Fifty years of children:
At first only planning and hoping,
Then the miracle of birth
And the joy of a child's chubby hand in ours;
Followed by the late nights and worrying
And the turbulence of adolescence;
And finally the pride and friendship of young men and women
Filled with strength—and strong in character.

Fifty years of giving and receiving,
Of disagreements and reconciliations,
Of patience and understanding,
Of joy and sorrows,
Of sharing,
Of love.

Fifty years of blessings—
To each other,
To family,
To those of us
Whose lives you have touched.

BRIDES AND GROOMS

❧

I admit it. I just love weddings. I love how each one is unique in reflecting the values and personalities of the bride and groom. I love how they bring families and friends together to celebrate the couple's start of their new life together. I love how beautiful the flowers are. I love how the light streams in from the stained-glass windows in church and how nice all the guests look in its glow. I love to see how handsome the groomsmen look and how beautiful the bridesmaids are. (As a sentimental soul with some pack-rat tendencies, I saved all my old bridesmaid dresses. They are still stuffed in the back of the closet.) And like everyone, I love to see how radiant and lovely the bride looks on her wedding day.

But there is one thing I love most about weddings, and not many people notice it. When the bride walks down the aisle and all eyes are on her, I watch the groom to see the look in his eyes and the smile on his face. When I see the look that says "She is such a blessing to me. I am the luckiest guy in the world that this beautiful, wonderful, amazing woman agreed to be my wife—and a lifetime is too short to show her how much I love her," then I know all is right.

I think the father of the bride hopes to see the same look. Because my next favorite thing I love about weddings is also something that many people skip over. When the bride and her father arrive at the front of the church where the groom is waiting for her, a sweet, magical, trusting moment takes place. A young woman's daddy, the man who has protected her, provided for her, been a role model for her, and loved her like the precious gift from heaven that she is, looks into the groom's eyes and entrusts his priceless treasure to him as he places his little girl's hand in his—trusting that the groom will continue to protect, provide, model good values and good behavior, and love her like her father does. So when the officiant speaks the ancient words and asks, "Who gives this woman to be wed to this man?", it is not surprising that her father can barely whisper out the words through tears: "I do."

The bride's father has always known that this heavenly gift is but for a few years. He has spent the last few precious moments walking her down the aisle. And in those moments, as Pachelbel's Canon in D has played, the videotape in his mind has played too: the day he brought her into the world; the evenings he walked in the door as she ran as fast as her little feet could carry her, flung her little arms around his legs, and squealed, "Daddy's home!"; and how quickly she went from braces and pigtails to evening gowns and makeup when the young woman standing before him in her first prom dress took his breath away. And at that moment, when his last walk with his little girl is over and the music stops, he realizes just how short his time with his precious gift has been. And he hopes beyond all hope that her new husband will treasure her and cherish her as much as he does.

Perhaps you too have given a daughter or a sister away, have wondered how the years could go by so quickly, and have known that a piece of your heart will always be missing. And you wish all of heaven's blessings would pour down on your sweet princess and her beloved.

When Kira, a lovely young friend of mine, and her fiancé, Gino, announced their engagement, I eagerly looked forward to her bridal shower and their wedding. I considered what to get for a bridal shower gift and perused her gift registry for ideas. I didn't want to get kitchenware or lingerie or china. Those things wear out over time. I wanted her to have the lifelong blessings of a wonderful marriage and home and family—the kind of blessings that are found in Proverbs 31: the blessings of a noble woman. I wanted her to have the divine blessings of the strong women of great faith throughout history—Sarah, Esther, Ruth, and Mary. And with the Holy Spirit's leading, and with pen in hand, I asked the Lord's timeless blessing on her and her beloved.

Her biological father was not at the wedding to give her away. But in God's great grace, her wonderful husband loved her through it. And when I recognized the look of love in his eyes as he waited for his bride, I knew that all would be well.

A GROOM'S BLESSING

Thank you for this man, O Lord.
May he be a man after your own heart.
As he enters into this sacred covenant,
May you finish in him the good works that you start.

May he seek and yearn after you, God,
May he be a reflection of his Father above.
Grant him humbleness, courage, and wisdom,
Prosperity, devotion, and love.

May he be the Protector of his Beloved,
May he be her safe place in the eye of the storm.
May he be her Provider and be generous in spirit,
May their home be loving, joyful, and warm.

May he lead his family to you, Lord,
By the living embodiment of a well-lived life.
May he hear your voice and follow your ways,
May he be a blessing to his children and wife.

May he treasure his Beloved as a treasure,
May he clothe her with praise and strength.
May his love for her be without measure,
May her respect for him be of unending length.

May he forever delight in his Beloved's embrace,
May their love be a seal over their hearts.
May their marriage be your sacred masterpiece, Father;
Their timeless love—your holy work of art.

A BRIDE'S BLESSING

O Princess of the King, radiant in your Wedding Dress,
Made by God's own Hand, breathed to Life by God's own Breath,
Your Wedding starts a journey as a Wife, Lover, and Friend.
May Blessings rain down on you, Noble Woman of Jehovah Elohim.

May you always be Beautiful, may you be Strong and Bold,
May your Life be filled with Grace as God's Great Women of Old:
Sarah, Esther, Mary, Ruth—
Great Women of Faith, Humble Women of Truth.

May your Faith be as Sarah's—Strong and Courageous,
May your Life leave a Legacy down through the Ages.
May you always be Thankful, may you give the Lord your best,
May you be forever Joyful, may you be forever Blessed.

May you be clothed as Ruth, with Strength and Dignity.
May your Life be marked by Righteousness, Goodness, and Charity.
May you be known for Graciousness, Kindness, and Love.
May God's own hand Protect you when you seek Refuge from Above.

May you lead with Wisdom, may your Mark never miss.
Like Esther, may God use you for such a Time as this.
May you answer his Call, whatever it may be,
May your heart be as Mary's—"Yes, Lord, use me."

May your husband Prosper, may his Wisdom and Stature raise,
May he delight in your Embrace, may he lift you with his Praise.
May your Home be full of Children, may your House be full of Joy,
May your Labors be always Fruitful, may you gain from your employ.

May God's Love reign in your Home, may your House be His Dwelling Place,
May your Marriage be the canvas upon which He paints his Amazing Grace.
As together you stand before God, as Ancient Words are spoken,
Bind yourselves with Love, for a cord of three strands is not easily broken.

May you know God's Voice and the touch of His Hand
And the breath of His Whisper and His Footprints upon the sand.
And now, as you go forth from this day as Husband and Wife,
May you and your Beloved share Love and share Life.

A BLESSING FOR MY HUSBAND

My Beloved, my Lover, my Husband, my Friend,
You are a cherished gift from Above.
In you I delight.
To you I have entrusted my heart.
I am my Beloved's, and my Beloved is mine.
Your banner over me is love.

Your strength protects me; your gentleness gives wings to my soul.
Your diligence provides for me; your playfulness fills me with laughter.
Your embrace heals me; your arms are my safe haven in the storm.
I blossom under the sweet, tender rain of your encouragement and kindness.
Place me as a seal upon your heart.

By your godly wisdom, you have built our home.
Through your understanding of God's ways, you have established our firm foundation.
And by your knowledge of that which is in this world, and that which is in the world beyond,
You have filled our home with precious treasures:
Our children, our families, our friends.
You invite the Lord to fill our home with his Presence.
Our family is blessed because of your goodness and righteousness.
You are our strong fortress and safe refuge.
In you we have a gentleman, a leader, a man of honor, a man after God's own heart—
You inspire us to walk in your ways.
Your humble walk with your Lord is a fountain of life for our family.

May you humbly seek the Lord, may your ways be gracious and bring glory to him.
May the Lord continue to bless you with wisdom and understanding, health and prosperity.
May the Lord uphold you and grant you strength of character in battle and kindness of spirit in peace.

May the God of your fathers go before you and behind you, above you and below you;
May your heavenly Father walk beside you and place his right hand on your shoulder to guide you.
May the joy of the Lord abound in your life, and the Lord of Life abound in your joy.
May the Spirit of the Most High abide in you and fill your soul.
May the Lord of Love surround you with the sweet affections of family and friends.
And may we dwell together in the House of the Lord and under the Shelter of his Wings,
As long as we both shall live.

A BLESSING FOR MY WIFE

My Beloved, my Lover, my Wife, my Friend,
In you I delight.
In you I have entrusted my heart.
I am my Beloved's, and my Beloved is mine.
My banner over you is love.

You have stolen my heart: I am enchanted by your exquisite beauty;
Your beauty within—a gentle and kind and peaceful spirit,
And your beauty without—loveliness without measure, the work of a Master Designer's hands.
My restless heart, adrift for so long, finds peace and contentment
In the safe harbor of your love.
I am held captive by your smile, resplendent and radiant as it warms my spirit.
Your tender touch and your gentle words heal my soul.
Angelshine surrounds you. Elegance and grace are yours.
In you, God has given me a treasured gift above all gifts.

By your noble character, you bless our family and honor me.
Through your godly wisdom, you have built our home.
By the timeless splendor of your spirit, you adorn our house with treasures of
Love, joy, peace, patience, kindness, gentleness, and compassion.
Encouragement is in your every word; goodness and righteousness are in your every deed.
Humility and generosity are in all you do.
You have made our home a safe sanctuary, a peaceful refuge from the storm.
Our children rise to bless you, and proudly claim you as their mother.
I can be the man God intended me to be with you by my side.

May the God of your fathers go before you and behind you, above you and below you:
May your heavenly Father walk beside you and place his right hand on your shoulder to guide you.
May the joy of the Lord abound in you, and the love of the Lord overflow in you.
May the Spirit of the Lord abide in you, and may you abide in him.
May you be surrounded with the sweet affections of family and friends.
May the blessings of God rain down upon you.
And may we dwell together in the House of the Lord and under the Shelter of his Wings
As long as we both shall live.

THE MYSTERY OF LOVE

How mysterious is the love between a man and a woman.
To be one, while encouraging the other to grow and delighting in each other's individuality.
To share the same goals and values, while being splendidly different.
To complement the other,
each with their own strengths and weaknesses,
so that together they are a whole.

To change the rest of one's life for the love of one man or one woman.
To expand the circle of love as the two become three.
To watch with deeper love and warmth,
as the mate one has chosen gently guides and loves the little ones,
made from love and God's breath of life,
the most precious of God's blessings.

To be both the best of friends and the best of lovers.
To care and be cared for,
need and be needed,
share and be shared with,
love and be loved.

To know love is a choice to act, not just an emotion to be felt.
To place the needs of others above the needs of oneself.

To watch love start as a flicker,
explode into a flame,
and gently turn into glowing embers
whose warmth lasts a lifetime.
Such is the wonderful mystery of the love between a man and a woman.

CHILDREN AND BABIES

"Babies are such a nice way to start people."
Don Herold

When my first child was born, I was overwhelmed with such a precious gift from God—he had used me as his vessel to create one of his miracles. Inside of me, the Ancient of Days had breathed his breath, and my child's spirit came to life. With each child, the wonder overwhelmed me anew. He formed their little bodies and personalities, and when they finally made their debuts, I was in awe of his masterpieces. What a privilege it was to be a coworker with the Maker of the Universe in forming such precious gifts! What a blessing to be entrusted with such treasures!

As I rocked them to sleep at night, I made up a lullaby for each one—a heart song, if you will—as I dreamed about how their futures would be. And as I cuddled them, I clung to those short, precious moments that we are allowed as parents before our children go out into the world and we must entrust them back to God's care. And thus began the children's blessings, lullabies, and heart songs that are included in this book.

Not too long after my dear friends Tom and Christiane, for whom I had written the wedding blessing, were married, they were expecting their first children—twins! What wonderful news! When trying to determine what to give for a baby present, I did not want to give something the twins would grow out of in a few short weeks, only to be put in the pile for the Salvation Army donations. Again, I wanted to give these beautiful children the things that every child needs—blessings from their Creator for a fulfilling life. And having walked this path myself, I wanted to give the new parents blessings so they would see their children through God's eyes (even when they write on the walls!) and raise their children in the love of the Lord.

"A Parent's Prayer" was born at the same time Thomas and Addison made their arrival. In essence, these are prayers of dedication, lifted up as we dedicate our children—God's children—to the Lord and dedicate ourselves to seeing them through God's eyes and surrounding them with the love and presence of God.

A PARENT'S PRAYER

Lord, thank you for these little ones
So fresh from your hand,
But we know our time with them goes quickly
Like the hourglass of sand.

And so we ask your blessings on us, new parents
Of these precious lives we share,
And give you thanks that you chose us
To entrust them to our care.

May we always see them through your eyes:
In your image—priceless treasures.
Help us teach them to follow your ways
So their inner beauty is of countless measure.

May we always hear them through your ears:
A joyful noise in every gurgle and cry.
Give us wisdom to teach them well
So their words glorify you on high.

May we always touch them with your arms:
Every hug a reminder of your love.
Give us patience, guide our path
As we raise these gifts from above.

Give us laughter in our home:
Giggles, plans, and schemes.
Give us faith and hope and love
And joy and delight and dreams.

And when we come to storms in life
As we no doubt will,
Help us lean on you, bring us close,
And your Spirit with us fill.

So rain down your blessings on us, O Lord,
And on your little ones so new,
For they are yours, but entrusted to us,
Before we give them back to you.

A BLESSING UPON OUR DAUGHTER

Precious One, O Little One, you are a daughter of the King,
A royal citizen of heaven. Herald angels announce your birth and sing:

"A princess of the King arrives! A unique child of God!
Fresh from God's own hand, from where the angels have trod.
Nowhere can she go where God's Spirit will not hear her.
The highest mountain, the deepest sea—even there, God is near her.
Wondrously God made her, in his image is she!
The Lord knew her name and ordained her days before one of them came to be."

You are a cherished treasure, a special gift from above
Entrusted to us for a short time, as we welcome you with love.
We thank the Lord for you, and we pray with one accord
That God rain down his blessings and that you come to know your Lord.

May the Lord God hold you in his kind and loving arms,
May he always protect you and keep you from all harm.
May you grow to be beautiful, strong, and courageous,
May your life leave a legacy down through the ages.

May you be known for your graciousness, kindness, and love,
May God grant you peace from heaven's gates above.
May you be clothed with righteousness, strength, and dignity,
May your life be marked by wisdom, joy, and charity.

May the Spirit of the Living God dwell richly in you,
May you seek the Lord's guidance in all you say and do.
May you know God's voice and the touch of his hand
And the breath of his whisper and his footprints upon the sand.

We pray an enduring prayer, we ask the Lord these things:
That he grant you faith and hope and love under the shelter of his wings.
And now, may you always walk with God, may your journey never end.
May you always call him "Lord" and may he ever call you "Friend."

A BLESSING UPON OUR SON

Precious One, O Little One, you are a son of the King,
A royal citizen of heaven. Herald angels announce your birth and sing:

"A prince of the King arrives! A unique child of God!
Fresh from God's own hand, from where the angels have trod.
Nowhere can he go where God's Spirit will not hear him.
The highest mountain, the deepest sea—even there, God is near him.
Wondrously God made him, in his image is he!
The Lord knew his name and ordained his days before one of them came to be."

You are a cherished treasure, a special gift from above
Entrusted to us for a short time, as we welcome you with love.
We thank the Lord for you, and we pray with one accord
That God rain down his blessings and that you come to know your Lord.

May you have the faith of Moses, from which you never depart.
When you stand on the shores of your Red Sea, may God make your seas part.
May your courage be that of Joshua, may you be strong and courageous,
May your life leave a legacy and speak to generations through the ages.

May your wisdom be as Solomon's, a guiding light in your life,
A source of wealth and prosperity, a beacon in times of strife.
May your heart beat as David's and proclaim "My God, how great thou art!"
May you seek the Lord, and may he call you "A man after my own heart."

May the Spirit of the Living God dwell richly in you,
May you seek the Lord's guidance in all you say and do.
May you know God's voice and the touch of his hand
And the breath of his whisper and his footprints upon the sand.

We pray an enduring prayer, we ask the Lord simply this:
That he might be on your side, and that you would always be on his.
And now, may you always walk with God, may your journey never end.
May you always call him "Lord," and may he ever call you "Friend."

MARTY'S LULLABY

Sweet Jesus loves you.
Your mama loves you.
Your daddy loves you more than you'll ever know.
So rock-a-bye, Sweet Child of Mine.

On the day that you were born
The angels danced for joy
To celebrate you coming to earth.
I counted your little fingers—and your little toes.
But I never expected to fall so much in love with you.

One day when you turn five, your first day of school,
You'll stand in front of that big ol' yellow bus.
Tousled golden hair,
Lunch box in your hand,
And then I will fall in love all over again.

Someday you'll be dressed all in black,
And she'll be your angel in white.
And when you look at her there will be stars in your eyes.
You'll put a ring on her finger
And tell her you'll always love her,
And then you will fall in love all over again.

One day you'll have one of your own
And the angels will dance for joy
To celebrate him coming to earth.
You'll count his little fingers
And his little toes,
Then you'll finally understand just how much I love you.

Sweet Jesus loves you,
Your mama loves you,
Your daddy loves you more than you'll ever know.
So rock-a-bye, Sweet Child of Mine.
I thank the Lord for letting me be your mom.

A MOTHER'S HEART SONG
(CHRISTY'S LULLABY)

Inside of me you were formed.
God knew you before you were born.
And for your mom he chose me,
Oh, how blessed can a woman be?
God chose me . . .

To have little arms around my neck
For little hugs; "Mommy, you're the best!"
For bedtime prayers upon our knees,
I've been blessed.

[for a girl]
Kindergarten, ponytails,
Tea parties, and fairy tales.
Senior prom, your wedding dress,
Heaven sent their angels' best.
I've been blessed.

[for a boy]
Blocks and bikes, snips and snails,
Trucks and trains and puppy tails.
Graduation day, you aced your test,
You chose a bride, invited guests.
I've been blessed.

Inside of me you were formed.
God knew us both before you were born.
He knew I needed you, he knew you needed me.
God blessed us both when he gave you to me.
Thank you, Lord, for choosing me.

FIRST MOTHER'S DAY

God performed another miracle today.

For months I prayed.

  I asked for his guidance.

    I asked for his will to be done.

For months I planned.

    As if the planning of an insignificant one such as me

        Had anything to do with God's ability to command a miracle,

          Just by his willing it so.

    But as a mere mortal, you must realize that I was compelled to do *something*

      To feel in control, which I most certainly am not.

For months I worried.

  About everything.

But today, it finally happened. God's own miracle.

  I, of course, can take no credit.

      I was merely an instrument

        In God's perfectly planned, harmonious, melodious,

       Sometimes discordant

         Symphony of Life—Act I.

I am most blessed!

  Because I was chosen as his vessel

    Into which he poured his love,

      Along with ample amounts of faith and hope.

  Because today I can only observe

    And watch with wonder

      The miracle unfold before my eyes.

  Because today I can admire

    The most precious handiwork

      Of the Master Designer.

I am most blessed!
    Because from this most unworthy and humblest of vessels,
        The Architect of the Universe chose to perform
            The most sacred of miracles:
                He created a new life.
I am most blessed!
    Because I hold her in my arms.

DONNY'S SONG

When you were just a boy, you played out with the bugs.
You played out in the mud. Then you came inside and gave me hugs.
"Mommy, I love you. Mommy, you're the best.
Mommy, do you like my bugs? Mommy, do you like my bird nest?"

I smiled and thought:
You're a part of me,
And I'm a part of you.
When you go out into the playground, remember:
      It's best to have a friend.
      Always to be kind.
      Disappointment is just a part of life.
      Hold on tight to God, your refuge and your strength.
      Don't be afraid to love, it will always come back to you.
      I don't know why, it's just true.

When you became a teen, loud music and blue jeans,
You put your arm around me and gave me a squeeze.
"Mom, I love you. I'll help you be cool.
Can I borrow your keys? We're hanging out after school."

I smiled and thought:
You're a part of me,
And I'm a part of you.
When you go out into high school, remember:
      It's best to have a friend.
      Always to be kind.
      Disappointment is just a part of life.

Hold on tight to God, your refuge and your strength.
Don't be afraid to love, it will always come back to you.
I don't know why, it's just true.

Now you stand before me a man with strength and dignity.
A leader with compassion and character of integrity.
"Mom, I love you. Thanks for coming to see me.
Let's go out to dinner. This time it's on me."

I smiled and I said, "I have a few things to say
Before you spread your wings and fly away:
You're a part of me,
And I'm a part of you.
When you go out into the world, remember:
    It's best to have a friend.
    Always to be kind.
    Disappointment is just a part of life.
    Hold on tight to God, your refuge and your strength.
    Don't be afraid to love, it will always come back to you.
    I don't know why, it's just true."

MAGIC MOMENTS

You came as a complete surprise.
    The news was quite unexpected.

Nevertheless, we prepared for your arrival with joyful anticipation—
    Cleaning, painting, shopping, and of course,
        Growing bigger every day.

When the day arrived, it was long.
    You weren't quite sure if you wanted to come—
        So you took your time.

When you finally decided to join us,
    Your protests were quieted when I gently called your name.
You see, you had heard me singing and talking to you for nine months.
    You knew my voice—and you knew your name.

You were exactly what I had asked God to send—
    A cute little fellow with blond hair, bright blue eyes,
        Full of snuggles and giggles and kisses.

The years have flown—
    Your first step,
        The first time you said "Mama,"
            A little golden head bouncing across of field of dandelions to give me a bouquet,
                Skipping stones together at the lake,
                    Snuggling under the covers on cold wintery Saturday mornings.

They are all magic moments stored forever as pictures in my memory bank.

I know the day will come.
  You will grow up and move away and have your own bouncing blondies.
    I will be but a visitor in your life.

But for now,
  You still put your little arms around my neck and say,
    "Mommy, you're the very best mommy in the whole wide world.
      I want to stay with you forever."

And, just for now, all is wonderful.

BAPTISM, CONFIRMATION, AND BIRTHDAYS

❧

A baptism is a landmark day in the life of a believer. Many church traditions have infant baptisms. These special occasions welcome new babies into the church family and are a time during which the parents dedicate themselves to raising their children in the love of God. Later, when the children are old enough to understand and have personally made a commitment to follow Christ, they confirm their faith in confirmation.

For most of my life, I have attended churches whose traditions celebrate what is called "believer's baptism." When a young person or adult wants to make a public affirmation of commitment to being a Christ-follower, he or she is dunked in a lake or baptismal pool at church, much like John the Baptist baptized people in the Jordan River. This full immersion into the water is symbolic of the complete washing of our sins as we rise to a new life in Christ.

When my youngest son, Marty, turned nine, he asked me if he could be baptized. From his first days, I could sense that he had a gentle spirit that God would use for good. Marty's first audible words were "tankoo" (thank you), and he spoke of God freely. So it was no surprise when he requested to be baptized. On a sunny day in August, he, along with a number of other members of our church ranging in age from six to sixty-six, were baptized in Lake Michigan, with the whole congregation cheering them on and giving them wet hugs as they emerged from the lake. Our lakeside baptism ceremony continues to be one of my favorite services of the year.

As I was reflecting on the importance of Marty's decision, I was reminded that Psalm 139 tells us that our names are written in God's book of life, and all our days are ordained before even one of them comes to be. God had Marty in mind and claimed him as his own from the beginning of time! I thought back to his first few weeks of life, when he contracted meningitis and we didn't know if we would have to give him back to God so soon. A few months later the doctor heard what he thought was a heart defect, and we feared that he would need open heart surgery at the tender age of one. We were relieved to find that God had just given his heart a different beat than the rest of us, and no surgery was needed.

I was reminded that my son's namesake, Martin Luther, stood before his accusers boldly proclaiming "With Christ I stand! I can do no other," and that he penned the enduring hymn, "A Mighty Fortress Is Our God." I knew there would be battles ahead, not just the physical kind, but spiritual battles—and I knew he would need all of God's armor to defeat the enemy and live a victorious, joy-filled life. And having sung "Amazing Grace" to him as his lullaby every night of his young life, I hoped that his life would reflect God's amazing grace in him and through him. "A Believer's Baptism Blessing" grew out of my reflections, and I gave him his own personalized version on the day he was baptized.

Although originally written for a baptism or confirmation, it is really a blessing for all of us who call upon the name of Christ, not just on the day we are baptized, but for all the days that we walk with God on this earth.

A BELIEVER'S BAPTISM BLESSING

Your name echoes through the ages, may you be strong and bold.
May your faith be steadfast and courageous, as the mighty saints of old.

Today you make a stand for Christ in front of many others.
"With Christ I stand," you proclaim, "I can do no other."
May he light a fire within you, and may you keep bright the flame,
Of the faith and hope and love that you find in Jesus' name.

May you put on the armor that you will need for the fight,
Of the battles unseen between wrong and right.
May the mighty belt of truth encircle your waist
And the breastplate of righteousness be firmly in place.

May your feet be swift to spread the gospel of peace,
May you pray in the Spirit, may your prayers never cease.
May your faith be strong, may it be your steadfast shield
And grant you victory over all the storms that life can wield.

May you don the helmet of God's sweet salvation,
May it protect you from harm and all of life's temptations.
May your only weapon be your two-edged sword
Of his Spirit within you, of the Word of the Lord.

May you be clothed head to toe with Jesus' great love,
May God pour down his blessings from heaven above.
May God use you as his vessel, may your soul be his dwelling place,
May your life be a canvas upon which God paints his amazing grace.

May you walk in righteousness where saints and angels have trod,
May you declare from the mountaintops: "A mighty fortress is our God!"
Your heart beats to a different drummer now, unlike all the rest,
May God's Spirit dwell deep within you and beat within your breast.

May your heart beat as one with Jesus as today a new life starts,
May you seek God, and may he call you "One after my own heart."
May you talk with your Lord daily, may he touch your heart anew,
May you be still and listen when he whispers to you.

We pray an enduring prayer, we ask God only this:
That he would be on your side and that you will always be on his.
May you always walk with Jesus. May your journey never end.
May you always call him "Lord," and may he forever call you "Friend."

AN INFANT'S BAPTISM BLESSING

Lord, we thank you for this little one
So fresh from your hand above.
We ask for your blessings upon him,
Our precious gift, made with love.

May the Cross of Christ alone
Seal his heart for eternity.
Father, Son, and Holy Spirit—
He is yours, blessed Trinity.

May his heart seek after yours.
May his faith grow strong.
May your grace fall fresh on him.
May he praise you with unending song.

Guide his path, light his way,
Lord, keep him close to you.
For you have entrusted him to us,
And now, we entrust him to you.

A BLESSING ON YOUR BIRTHDAY

May you seek the Lord's guidance
In all that you do.
May you follow him
And to Christ only be true.

May you be in his Word
Day after day.
May he bless you and keep you
In so many ways.

May you lean on his strength
When the storms of life blow.
May you seek his forgiveness
And be washed white as snow.

May you praise him and thank him
And burst into song.
May he bless you, his dear friend,
All your life long.

A BLESSING AS YOU CONFIRM YOUR FAITH

As you confirm your faith,
As you accept the Gift of Grace God has imparted,
May God finish within you
The good work that he has started.

May Love, Joy, and Peace
Be imprinted upon your heart.
May Patience, Kindness, and Goodness
Be your end and be your start.

May Faithfulness, Gentleness, and Self-Control
Be the virtues for which you are known.
May you sow seeds of goodness,
May you reap what you have sown.

May you cloak yourself in Humbleness.
May Wisdom be your Guide.
May you daily seek to know your Lord
And in his Love abide.

May his Spirit dwell within you.
May your soul be God's dwelling place.
May your life be the Masterpiece
Upon which God paints his Amazing Grace.

As you confirm your Faith,
As you go where Saints before you have trod,
May you seek his face and know his Grace
And walk humbly with your God.

A BLESSING ON YOUR FIRST COMMUNION

As you join the communion of saints,
As you partake in your first communion,
May you proclaim the Lord's sacrifice until he comes—
Until our blessed reunion.

As you eat the Bread of Life
May you remember his Love for you.
As you drink the cup of wine
May you claim his promises as True.

"I will never leave you or forsake you.
I am with you always.
Seek me first, love your God and your brother
And I will guide your ways."

As you join the fellowship of believers,
You start a journey without end.
May you always walk with the Lord your God,
And may he always call you friend.

MILITARY BLESSINGS

I grew up on Chanute Air Force Base in Rantoul, Illinois. My dad had been an infantryman in World War II and was a civilian instructor on the base. Although I'd always had a great respect for our men and women in uniform, after Dad and I retraced his footsteps through Europe on the sixtieth anniversary of D-Day and reconnected with lifelong friends whose lands he had liberated, my respect moved from my head to deep within my heart. The journal I kept of our sojourn eventually became a book, *Angels of Ebermannstadt.*

The kinship shared among soldiers, sailors, Marines, and airmen who have been in combat—this band of brothers—is a bond unlike any other. Within a few short months of joining the service, they grow from immature, video-gaming boys full of bravado and hubris to men of honor willing to sacrifice their very lives for their country and the members of their platoon.

The term "Band of Brothers" was originally coined by Shakespeare in his play Henry V and known as the Saint Crispian's Day Speech. On the eve of the Battle of Agincourt in 1415, the English knights were outnumbered and discouraged by the militarily superior French. Henry V spoke from his heart, appealed to the honor of his men, and encouraged his troops with what is still considered one of the most motivating speeches in history, calling his men, "We few, we happy few, we band of brothers; For he today that sheds his blood with me shall be my brother." The small English army was victorious over the French. This timeless speech is included here in honor of our own Band of Brothers, the United States military.

These blessings weave in the traditions, hymns, and history of each branch of our military and ask the Lord's hand of protection over the brave men and women who defend our country on these sacred shores and those abroad. May we be forever grateful to those who sacrifice so much, and in return, ask for so little.

AN AIRMAN'S BLESSING

When off you go
Into the wild blue yonder,
May the Lord fly with you,
Wherever you may wander.

May integrity, service, excellence
Be written on your heart.
Fly, fight, win!
It's where you end and where you start.

May your Band of Brothers
Never falter, never fail.
Wingman, leader, and sentry—
In every mission, may you prevail.

Heart of a warrior, soul of a patriot,
Lover of your country and your God,
Honor and valor go before you,
Guardian of freedom, at home and abroad.

May your heart be forever brave,
May you be strong and courageous.
You have answered your nation's call,
As you forge a legacy for the ages.

For the flags of our fathers,
For the freedom of our sons,
May you return safely
When the battle is won.

May your mark be always true,
May Jehovah be ever by your side,
May the Lord be your steadfast shield,
May his Spirit be your unwavering guide.

A MARINE'S BLESSING

From the halls of Montezuma
To the shores of Tripoli,
May the heavenly hosts protect you
On the air, on land, and sea.

May honor, courage, commitment
Be written on your heart
Much more than a motto:
It's where you end and where you start.

May your Band of Brothers
Be a brotherhood indeed:
A few good men, defenders of liberty,
Protectors of those in need.

Heart of a warrior and soul of a patriot,
Lover of your country and your God.
Honor and tradition go before you
As you march where other Marines have trod.

May your heart be forever brave,
May you be strong and courageous.
May the Lord go before you,
As you forge a legacy for the ages.

For the flags of our fathers,
For the future of our sons,
May you return home safely
When the battle is won.

May the Lord be your steadfast shield;
His Spirit your unwavering guide.
May your mark be always true.
God bless the Marines. Semper fi!

A SAILOR'S BLESSING

As you sail to foreign shores,
As you anchors aweigh,
May God's breath fill your sails
When you sail at break of day.

May honor, courage, commitment
Be written on your heart.
Much more than a motto,
It's where you end and where you start.

May your Band of Brothers
Hear your nation's call
With faith, courage, and service
And honor over all.

Heart of a warrior, soul of a patriot,
May you be victorious and prevail!
Tradition and honor go before you
As you voyage where sailors before you have sailed.

May your heart be forever brave,
May you be strong and courageous,
As you navigate the oceans,
And forge a legacy for the ages.

In the blue of the mighty deep,
May you be protected by God's own Son,
Until we meet once more on these sacred shores
When the battle is won.

May the Lord be ever by your side.
This is our unending plea:
May his Spirit be your shelter and guide
As you sail the seven seas.

A SOLDIER'S BLESSING

As you fight for the right
With the cadence loud and strong,
May the heavenly hosts protect you
As the Army goes rolling along.

May duty, honor, country
Be written on your heart.
Much more than a motto,
It's where you end and where you start.

May your Band of Brothers
Be a brotherhood indeed.
This we'll defend!
Liberty, justice, and those in need.

Heart of a warrior, soul of a patriot,
With faith in your country and your God.
Tradition and honor go before you
As you march where soldiers before you have trod.

May your heart be forever brave,
May you be strong and courageous,
As you fight with all your might
For a legacy through the ages.

For the flags of our fathers,
For the freedom of our sons,
May you return home safely
When the battle is won.

May Jehovah be ever by your side,
May your faith in God be strong.
May his Spirit be your guide
As the caissons go rolling along.

A PRAYER ON MEMORIAL DAY

May we always revere the sweetness of liberty,
    And forever appreciate the high price at which it comes.

May we always treasure our freedom to speak freely,
    And forever sanctify the blood shed so that we may have the right to protest.

May we always cherish our ability to worship God according to the dictates of our conscience,
      And forever pay tribute to our Christian forefathers who gave us the freedom to reject the very
         God who blesses us.

May we walk the verdant fields lined with white crosses and Stars of David
In quiet reverence of those who died so that we may live,

And may we teach of their last full measure of love and devotion to their God and their country
To our children and our children's children.

Amen.

BAND OF BROTHERS

If we are mark'd to die, we are enow
To do our country loss; and if to live,
The fewer men, the greater share of honour.
God's will! I pray thee, wish not one man more.
By Jove, I am not covetous for gold,
Nor care I who doth feed upon my cost;
It yearns me not if men my garments wear;
Such outward things dwell not in my desires.
But if it be a sin to covet honour,
I am the most offending soul alive.
No, faith, my coz, wish not a man from England.
God's peace! I would not lose so great an honour
As one man more methinks would share from me
For the best hope I have. O, do not wish one more!
Rather proclaim it, Westmoreland, through my host,
That he which hath no stomach to this fight,
Let him depart; his passport shall be made,
And crowns for convoy put into his purse;
We would not die in that man's company
That fears his fellowship to die with us.
This day is call'd the feast of Crispian.
He that outlives this day, and comes safe home,
Will stand a tip-toe when this day is nam'd,
And rouse him at the name of Crispian.
He that shall live this day, and see old age,
Will yearly on the vigil feast his neighbours,
And say "To-morrow is Saint Crispian."
Then will he strip his sleeve and show his scars,

And say "These wounds I had on Crispian's day."
Old men forget; yet all shall be forgot,
But he'll remember, with advantages,
What feats he did that day. Then shall our names,
Familiar in his mouth as household words—
Harry the King, Bedford and Exeter,
Warwick and Talbot, Salisbury and Gloucester—
Be in their flowing cups freshly remember'd.
This story shall the good man teach his son;
And Crispin Crispian shall ne'er go by,
From this day to the ending of the world,
But we in it shall be remembered—
We few, we happy few, we band of brothers;
For he to-day that sheds his blood with me
Shall be my brother; be he ne'er so vile,
This day shall gentle his condition;
And gentlemen in England now-a-bed
Shall think themselves accurs'd they were not here,
And hold their manhoods cheap whiles any speaks
That fought with us upon Saint Crispin's day.
—William Shakespeare, *Henry V*

A number of years ago, I had the honor of being asked by a national organization to say the invocation for a luncheon honoring Steve Forbes, the financial guru and editor of Forbes Magazine who explains in plain English what is happening in our economy and financial markets to the rest of us who are befuddled when our retirement accounts drop by half in one day. In the past, invocations for this patriotic organization had inadvertently excluded certain religious groups, and I was asked to be mindful and inclusive of both Christian and Jewish traditions in my prayer. As always, I asked the Holy Spirit that the words be his words, not mine. Thankfully, when we ask the Spirit for his words, he is faithful to answer us.

While the original prayer was for a specific event, with some tweaking, I have included it here so that it can be used for any event in which we ask the Lord's blessings upon our country.

A PRAYER TO BLESS OUR NATION

Heavenly Father, Adonai—our Lord, El Elyon—God Most High, El Shaddai—God Almighty, you indeed are the Giver of all good gifts. We come before you today with thankful hearts for the bounty you have provided and for the country in which we are privileged to live. We recognize that our forefathers founded this land on your guiding principles and, "with a firm reliance on the protection on Divine Providence," sought your blessings on our fledgling country. You have blessed us beyond measure and we give you thanks.

Father, we gather here today because of our concern for the welfare of our great nation. In your Word, Solomon tells us that fear of the Lord is the beginning of knowledge, and to seek Wisdom and Understanding from you. Therefore, we humbly come before you to give us the godly wisdom to make the right recommendations to our political leaders. Help us to do justice to the principles of liberty that established these United States of America. Remind us, in the midst of whatever problems we seek to solve, what a blessing it is to be a part of this grand experiment in political freedom.

Through your prophet Micah, you tell us that you require us to act justly, love mercy, and walk humbly with our God. And so we ask you, in your graciousness, to help us be just and merciful, to be a lamp to our path and a light to our way, to guide us and hold us fast with your right hand, and, each day, to make us more like your image. May our words and actions reflect your grace.

Lord, bless this gathering. May your Spirit be present in our fellowship together. We thank you for our leaders, for the positive impact they have made on this country, and for the wisdom and many gifts you have bestowed upon them. Bless them and their work. May we all have ears to hear and eyes to see that which you would have us understand.

Father, we ask your blessings upon our nation and your wisdom upon our leaders. We pray America's enduring prayer—not that you would be on our side, but that we might always be on yours.

It is in your mighty name, Jehovah, that we pray. Amen.

HOME AND FAMILY

❧

One of the best things about growing up and moving out is coming back home. Whether small or large, modern or traditional, simple or fancy, home makes us feel grounded and content. It is much more than just a building. Home is the one unique place designed by God to be a safe haven from the storms of life, a sanctuary where we are nurtured and able to grow, an incubator of joy and life and love with the ones we care about most. It's the place where our parents give us roots to grow and wings to fly. And at the proper time—usually about three years later than teenagers want and ten years earlier than parents think they are ready—we leave our childhood home to start our own.

At ninety-four, my mom still owns the house that I grew up in, the house she and my dad bought in 1966. It was one hundred years old then—it's ancient and empty now—but she can't bear to part with it just yet, and honestly, I'm not so sure I'm ready either. That house tugs on my heartstrings and makes me long for days that are past—when my parents were healthy and my children excitedly looked forward to spending time with Grandma and Grandpa.

When I visit my hometown, a one-stoplight town in the middle of an Illinois cornfield, I always stop to check in on my childhood home. Every room has stories to tell and memories of lessons I have learned. As I park on the street and walk across the front yard, I look to make sure the tree house that my dad built in the crab apple tree is still there for the neighborhood kids to play on. My old tree house taught me that getting away to nature and a good tree is calming for the soul. I walk up the front steps and remember sitting on them in warm summer evenings with a boyfriend who serenaded me with his guitar. I learned that sitting next to your sweetheart just talking and singing is one of life's greatest joys.

When I open the front door that only unlocks if you jiggle the key a little to the left and then tug, I almost expect to hear familiar voices welcoming us, and I breathe in the smell of home. I learned that being a good hostess means making people feel welcome. The family room with the old upright piano that Dad bought from the neighbors for fifty dollars (after my begging for a piano for two years) is where I learned to love music.

The little quarter-sawn oak dining table that has been in my mom's family for over one hundred years has stories to tell of every family dinner, every Thanksgiving, every Christmas for five generations. Dad spoke the same prayer before each meal as we held hands and reconnected at the end of the day with the ones we loved. I learned that, regardless of conflicts we may have with each other, love endures; and coming together for a meal, holding hands, and asking God to be in our midst feeds the body and the soul.

The kitchen that Dad built for Mom was the hub of activity—my mom could putter there for hours making apple pies and apple cakes and apple anything from Dad's prized apples trees in the backyard. I sit on the kitchen stool and can see Dad pouring a cup of the best coffee in the world as we chat about the latest workshop project he is working on, or how he helped Farmer Guynn fix his tractor, or the fun we had on one of our "Dick and Charlie's Excellent Adventures," or my latest life dilemma. I learned that it is good to stay busy, to help others, and to have fun, and I learned that there are few problems that cannot be solved over a cup of hot coffee and warm apple pie served with a side of wisdom.

On the kitchen wall across from the old black dial telephone are pencil lines and dates that mark our heights growing up, plus those of all my children. I learned that it's good to celebrate life's little milestones. My bedroom (still in that hideous orange from the seventies) is full of my treasures—dresses that Mom made, souvenirs that Dad bought to remember our family vacations, awards and photos and letters and cards. The upper left-hand drawer of my dresser still holds the crumpled love notes written by the young gentleman who serenaded me on the front steps. My room still has the little twin bed that Mom and I sat on when I poured out my heart to her over a skinned knee or a broken heart. I learned that it is good to be sentimental, and that when someone hurts, you should give them a hug, two open ears, and a tissue. The backyard has an old tire swing that Grandpa put on the walnut tree for his grandkids. I learned that there is a special bond between grandparents and grandchildren—and both are the better for it. My loyal four-footed childhood companion, Smokey, is buried near the fence under the tombstone my dad made for her: "Smokey: Always Faithful." I learned that if people were as loving and loyal as most dogs, the world would be a better place.

My dad never hired people to do things that he could do himself. I learned to be self-reliant and resourceful just by watching him. And since he could do everything himself, and because he loved her so much, he loved making our house the home my mom always wanted. By watching them live life together, I learned what love looks like. When they bought the house, my mom loved the house, but not the location. So my dad bought the lot she liked, built a basement and foundation, and literally moved the house across town.

I pause a moment to look at the garage he built—he had his workshop there, and WGN radio was always on, telling us the latest on everything from the farm report to the Cubbies. In the garage, I learned how to use every tool known to man, I learned all about baseball, and I learned that, in the workshop and in life, it is best to measure twice and cut once. The brick patio that I helped Dad put in one summer when it was 102 degrees in the shade is now covered with weeds, and the lilac tree he planted for Mom is a bit unruly and overgrown. I learned to finish a job, regardless of how hard it is. Summertime meant outdoor summer projects (unpaid, of course), and I was assigned the task one summer of painting the entire fence (a la Tom Sawyer) and the next summer of painting the house. I learned that houses, along with everything else we care about in life from cars to relationships, need to be lovingly maintained.

I was reminded of the words of Solomon, who once said, "Unless the Lord builds the house, those who build it labor in vain" (Proverbs 127:1). God wants to be right in the midst of our homes and our families so that he can bless us and be part of our lives. So that our earthly homes can be a little microcosm of what our heavenly home looks like. As I walked around my childhood home, I was thankful that my folks asked God to be their general contractor.

It occurred to me, as a whole host of memories and colliding emotions came bursting in, as perhaps it has occurred to you while visiting your childhood home, that my parents built not just a house, but a home. And that home built me.

So when my friends John and Paula bought their first house together, I thought of all the blessings that each room of their new home would bring to them and their family. I thought of all the wonderful memories that would be made in that house. And I prayed that hearts would be knit together and that lives would be lovingly built in that place. Out of those good wishes and prayers, a house blessing emerged.

Their framed home blessing now hangs by their front door to remind them that they are building a house with God, and to welcome and bless all who enter.

A HOUSE BLESSING

May your door be always open to family and friends,
May your foundation be solid rock in a world of sand.
May your roof be a shelter from the storms of life,
May your windows bring fresh breezes off the land.

May your kitchen be the heart of your home
Serving good food and good cheer.
May it nourish the body and the soul,
May it bless all who enter here.

May friends gather 'round your table
With laughter, food, and wine.
May precious memories of the life you share
Be made in the rooms where you dine.

May the bedrooms be the safe haven that renews
Tired bodies and tired minds.
May sweet, sweet rest and gentle sleep
Bring refreshment and renewal sublime.

May New Year's Eve and Christmas Day
And all the celebrations in between
Tie your hearts together with Love
With cherished memories yet to be seen.

May the language of Love be spoken here
And the gift of Grace freely given.
May the Lord fill your Home with Faith, Hope, and Love
On earth, may it be a glimpse of heaven.

A NEW HOME DEDICATION

Lord, thank you for this new home.
It is a gift from you!
Thank you, thank you, thank you!

Give us your Spirit of boldness and confidence
And joy and love.
Don't let us look back with regrets or what-ifs,
But let us look forward boldly to what you will do.

We dedicate this home to you to use as you will.
May it be filled with
Love
Joy
Peace
Patience
Kindness
Goodness
Gentleness
Faithfulness
Self-Control, and
Wisdom.

May you lead people to it whom you want to be touched by your Spirit.
May you use us to touch them.
Bring peace and prosperity to all who enter.

Fill us with your Spirit to do your good works here on earth.
    May we be your hands and feet.
        May family and friends find this home
            A sweet refuge
              And peaceful sanctuary.

May your Presence fill us
    And may all who enter feel your Presence.

May your healing love heal wounded hearts
    So that they are full of your love
        And overflow with love for others.

So Lord, we thank you for this home,
    A gift from you.
        Remind us that we are stewards of this gift,
            As we are stewards of all your good gifts,
            And remind us that this is your home,
                Provided to us to do your good works. Amen.

THE MUSIC OF MY FAMILY

Some families are classical music—
    Each cadence strictly measured,
        Each note prudently planned,
            Each measure carefully written.

Some families are country music songs—
    Recalling unfortunate times,
        Dwelling on sad moments,
            A story of endless struggle.

Some families are rap music—
    A constant flow of talk,
        Hurtful and hateful,
            Angry and despairing.

My family is a jazz music jam session—
    A jubilant, unwritten expression of joys and sorrows,
        One unending song with solo improvisations,
            The unorchestrated ebb and flow of life in presto and andante.

OUR FAMILY PRAYER

May we Love
Even when others are unlovely.
May we multiply each other's Joys
And divide each other's Sorrows.

May our home be a haven of Peace
In the midst of the storms of life.
May we be Patient and Understanding,
Especially when the other needs it most.

May Kindness be imprinted
Upon all our words and deeds.
May Goodness and Righteousness be our mark,
Even when they are unpopular.

May Wisdom be a light unto our way
And a lamp to guide our path.
May we each Delight in our Beloved
And be forever captivated by the love of our youth.

May Self-Restraint and Faithfulness be our guide
In the midst of life's temptations.
May Health and Prosperity follow us
Wherever we may go.

May Laughter and Friends and Family
Always fill our home.
May Forgiveness and Graciousness be freely given
And humbly accepted.

May we live to see our Children's Children,
And may they rise up and call us Blessed.
May we seek the Lord's Guidance
In all that we do and in all that we say.

May our Family be a reflection of God's Love.
And may we dwell in God's Grace
And under the Shelter of His Wings
As long as we shall live.

A BLESSING FOR MY FATHER

Thank you for being my Hero,
For teaching me Right from Wrong.
Thank you for always Protecting me
With your Embrace—both Loving and Strong.

Thank you for your timeless Wisdom
And not telling me how to live,
But Patiently teaching by your Example
Of Living a Life Well-lived.

Thank you for your Gentle Guiding Hand
And always being Proud of me,
For showing me what Character looks like:
Kindness, Hard Work, and Integrity.

Thank you for your Gift of Faith
And being a Righter of Wrongs.
And for Adventures, and Quests and Cowboys,
And being a Singer of Songs.

Thank you for always fixing things
From broken Hearts to broken toy trains,
Using skillful Hands and big bear hugs,
And hammers and levels and planes.

My Greatest Gift has been you, Dad,
Chosen especially for me from Above;
An earthly Father—an endless Heart,
Reflecting my Heavenly Father's endless Love.

A LETTER TO GOD ON FATHER'S DAY

Dear God,

I can't say thanks enough for giving me the father you gave me. He was a perfect fit—of course (you know both of us so well!). He wasn't rich or powerful, but he was the perfect dad for me. He didn't teach me everything in life, but he taught me the most important things. (Thankfully, you filled in the rest.) And he taught most of them without even telling me, or lecturing me, but by his example.

He taught me:

Friends are just strangers you haven't met yet.

Always be loyal to a friend—they aren't perfect and neither are you, but you can still be good friends.

Be honest.

One of the greatest joys in life is helping other people, so look for ways to help—mow a neighbor's yard, shovel a widow's driveway, be a handyman to a single mom, read to a class of children, be a mentor to a younger person.

If you are nice to people, they are generally nice back—if not, don't bother with them.

Forgiveness is a good thing.

Everybody needs hugs.

Get to know your kids' friends and their families—there's a good chance they will become your friends too.

Going to church is a good thing, but living by the Golden Rule is even better.

It's good to have friends of all different backgrounds, interests, and ages.

Having coffee with your old buddies every morning at a local diner is good for the soul.

So is ice cream.

Love your wife like she is the special treasure that God gave you. Compliment her often—in front of the kids, in public, and just when you are alone.

Never let your girls put limitations on their aspirations just because they are girls.

Teach girls to use power tools and work on trucks.

Keep in touch with people—write lots of letters.

Don't start fights—but if you are in one, fight hard.

Teach girls not to be afraid of spiders or mice or other critters.

It's okay to be friendly and talk to strangers—you can meet the most interesting people that way.

Appreciate your spouse and his or her qualities, even if you are two very different people.

Have a good belly laugh at least once a day.

Don't say bad things about people—most people are just trying their best.

When you pray, do it to an audience of One.

If you get an invitation to do something fun, just say "yes" and don't worry about the rest.

Keep active no matter how old you get.

Support your kids and let them know they are loved.

If they threaten to run away—offer to go with them.

Have fun.

It doesn't matter how many degrees you have behind your name or what you do for a living, as long as it's a good honest living.

And whatever you do—whether you are a professional or a ditchdigger—do the very best you can, so that if you are a ditchdigger, you'd better be the best darn ditchdigger there is.

Be humble.

Be thankful.

Lord, thank you for sending me a dad so much like you. Happy Father's Day.

A BLESSING FOR MY MOTHER

Thank you for teaching me Right from wrong;
Thank you for your Wisdom and Grace.
Thank you for your Patient Instruction
And letting me learn from my mistakes.

Thank you for giving me Confidence
That real Beauty comes from within:
A Joyous Spirit, Kindness toward all,
Love and Laughter with Family and Friends.

Thank you for showing me what Strength looks like—
No, not the brutish form—
But the quiet kind that comes from siding with Right
And standing Steadfast in the Storm.

Thank you for making thousands of Meals
And sharing your Faith, which has made me whole.
With heads bowed in Prayer and served with Love,
You fed my Body, Spirit, and Soul.

Thank you for showing me what Love looks like
With your unending Sacrifice for me,
And for helping me grow and letting me go
When it was my Time to leave.

May God shower his Blessings upon you,
His Special Angel sent from above.
For I am who I am because of you
And because of your Great Love.

A BLESSING UPON MY SISTER

May the goodness that is in you blossom and grow
And bless all who are around you.
May goodness and good people
Bless you and surround you.

May confidence in yourself and in your God
Grow from day to day.
May your faith be strong and bold and brave
To carry you on adventures each day.

May the Lord crown your efforts with success,
May you find joy in the work you choose.
May your arms be always open to the needy and poor,
May a generous spirit show in all you do.

May strength and dignity be your cloak,
May you laugh in all the days that come.
May your words be filled with wisdom and grace,
May faithful instruction be on your tongue.

May God's protection and provision be upon you
In a home filled with joy and peace.
May encouragement and praise be freely given,
May the love of family never cease.

May the radiant beauty that is within you
Shine forth as it transcends
Your wonderful beauty on the outside,
My sister and my friend.

SAGES AND SENIORS

❧

When my parents were in their eighties, I saw forty come and go, and I realized that my life was already half-lived. I felt moved by the Spirit to write a prayer of thanks for them while I was on a mission trip in Mexico. As members of the Greatest Generation, they lived through a Depression. When war broke out, even though he was only seventeen, my father fibbed about his age so he could enlist. My mother's heart was moved when she learned of the mistreatment of Japanese-Americans, and as a young teacher, she moved to Wyoming and taught school in the Japanese internment camp at Heart Mountain with her best friend, Charlene Pease (my namesake). They longed for peace and justice and were compelled to right wrongs. As the apostle Paul tells us to do, they let their lives be a living sacrifice.

Like so many others, after the war, my parents married and settled into a peaceful life of raising a family, working hard, instilling their godly values in the next generation, and serving others.

I think many of us don't fully appreciate our parents until we have children of our own. I am guilty of that. As they entered the sunset of their lives and I entered the autumn of mine, I was finally able to appreciate how blessed I was to have them as my mom and dad and as grandparents to my children—to have them inside of me and my children. They continued to be my best teachers by their selfless examples of lives well-lived.

"The Octogenarians" was a heart song that emerged as I reflected on these things. Years later, as I contemplated the countless acts of service performed by their hands, from the days of their childhood until the day the Lord called them home, I was led again by the Spirit to write "Bless These Hands."

I am mindful that not everyone who grows older grows wiser. Unless we make an intentional effort to become more like God by spending time in his Word, allowing his words to shape our souls, humbling ourselves in acts of service, talking to him in prayer, and quieting our lives so that we may listen when he whispers to us, we don't grow older and wiser. We just grow older. As we grow in our faith journey, we all need a Paul and a Timothy in our lives. We need a wise, older person who has walked the path before us and who invests time in us, and we need a younger person seeking to grow in faith and wisdom by looking to us as an example. We need both mentors and mentees.

May we always be thankful for the wise, elder sages that God puts in our lives to lead us in his ways by their loving example. And as we grow older, may God allow us to grow in wisdom and grace so that we may be the counselor, the mentor, the elder friend who gently guides our younger brothers and sisters on their paths toward him.

THE OCTOGENARIANS

The Octogenarians—
They are a bit slower than the rest of us.
They have run their race—and they have won.
They have heard the words, "Well done, my good and faithful servant."
They are now walking their victory lap.

The Octogenarians—
They are a bit more thankful than the rest of us.
They have endured the Depression with hole-ridden shoes and hungry stomachs.
They have survived a war—crawling on their bellies with the blood of a fallen soldier and friend
splattered on their fatigues.
They have witnessed injustice—and were compelled to right a wrong.
Yet their hearts have been moved by the kindness of strangers,
the warmth of friendship, the love of family.
They have seen the worst mankind has to offer—and the best.
And still, they are thankful.
They have no time to dwell on that which has not been given;
they are much too occupied being thankful for that which has.

The Octogenarians—
Their love of their country is a bit stronger than the rest of ours.
Their commitment runs deep within their soul.
They are as much a part of America as America is a part of them.
When war called—they answered,
Knowing, as their forefathers before them, that the liberty this country offers
can only be purchased with the precious blood
of those willing to die for freedom.

The Octogenarians—
They are a bit more content than the rest of us.
Their serenity shows in the twinkle of their eyes and in the peace on their countenance.
They have been in the midst of wealth, they have seen unthinkable poverty.
Yet they have found the secret to contentment in every situation.

The Octogenarians—
They are a bit wiser than the rest of us.
Years of experiences have given them insight into the human soul.
They know that the fear of the Lord is the first step towards wisdom.
And they have reaped the blessings of a life lived with wisdom and grace and righteousness.

The Octogenarians—
They are a bit more like God than the rest of us.
Just like children, so fresh from the hand of God, are God-like,
So, too, are the octogenarians, as our Lord draws them closer to home—and to him.

The Octogenarians—
Are they a bit more blessed than the rest of us?
I think not.
For it is I who am blessed
Because I was chosen to be their child.
For it is I who am blessed
Because I am a part of them.
For it is I who am blessed
Because they are in me.

BLESS THESE HANDS

Bless these old hands, so wrinkled and red.
What a journey they've had, what a life they have led.

Bless these hands that once used to skip stones,
Held a new puppy, helped him dig for bones.
Bless these hands that played ball and sports,
Cheered on the team, had fun of all sorts.

Bless these hands that hold my sweetheart dear,
An angel from heaven brought to me here.
Bless these hands that wear the ring of the love of my life,
Cherished and adored, we became husband and wife.

Bless these hands that held our new babes made from love,
Miracles, joys, precious gifts from above.
Bless these hands that wiped away little tears
And gave big bear hugs and kissed away fears.

Bless these hands that taught my son to ride
A trike, then a bike, then an old Jeep to drive.
Bless these hands that gave my daughter away
To a husband, a new life, and children someday.

Bless these hands that have worked oh, so hard,
On the farm, in the plant, pulling weeds in the yard,
Deadlines and due dates and papers to send,
Dishes and laundry and meals without end.

Bless these hands that have held both a gun and a plough,
Have been folded in prayer, wiped sweat from my brow.
Bless these hands that have made a good living
With more than I need, so I could give and keep giving.

Bless these hands that have comforted a friend
With a hug or a touch or a card that was sent.
Bless these hands that have spread joy and good cheer
With a handshake, a hug, and a "How are you, dear?"

You gave me these hands, Lord, to use them for good:
"Be my hands here on earth, use them as I would.
For I have no hands on earth but yours
For healing hearts, for opening doors."

These hands are older and wrinkly now
But your Spirit tells me they are lovely somehow.
Thank you, Lord, for these hands, what gifts they have been.
What a privilege to be your hands on earth. Amen.

BLESSINGS FOR THOSE WHO BLESS US

I love how God puts special people in our lives to encourage us when we are disheartened, challenge us when we need redirection, heal us when we have been wounded, love us to make our souls sing, protect us from what can be a dangerous world, and help us grow more like him. And oftentimes, he puts *us* in others' lives to encourage, challenge, heal, love, and protect them, and to help them grow into the people God designed them to be. When God has someone in mind whom he needs us to meet, or who needs to meet us, and then arranges the meeting, I call all of these not-so-chance intersections and meetings "divine appointments."

What would our lives look like if, for every person we crossed paths with, we saw through God's eyes and we asked the Holy Spirit, "Why did God put him in my path today? What would God have me say to him? What would God have me hear from him?" What would it look like if we really listened as the Holy Spirit whispered to us? *Yes, Joe is a bit grumpy. And his clothes are disheveled and he needs a shave. He just lost his job, and he is so discouraged. I arranged for you to bump into him at the gas station today to encourage him and to tell him about the job opening at your company.* Or perhaps the Spirit might say, *You're right, Susie isn't paying attention in class this week. She is a million miles away. She has an abusive father who tells her she's worthless. I put her in your classroom so you would inspire her and love on her and make her believe that she can be the doctor I have called her to be.* Or, as a friend shared with me recently, *The doctor who is examining you has just had her area of practice eliminated at this hospital and is contemplating a major career change. She needs to hear from you that she is called to be a healer, after the Great Physician, and is headed in the right direction.*

I thank God for the people he places in our families, our circles of friendship, our places of work, and in our churches, schools, and communities who shape us and mold us. Sometimes they walk with us for just a season, and sometimes for a lifetime. Each of these blessings celebrates some of those divine appointments in our lives.

A TEACHER'S BLESSING

May you be inspired by the lives you inspire.
May your heart be encouraged by the young people you encourage.
May your students believe in you as much as you believe in them.
May you be shown patience as you patiently show others.

May wisdom be yours as you weave lifelong lessons
Amongst the poetry and history and philosophy.
May your words be filled with grace to touch their hearts
As you open their minds.
And may your heart be full of kindness
Because they don't care how much you know
Until they know how much you care.

May you know joy as you bring the love of learning to the classroom.
May you travel to distant lands as literature and languages spring to life.
May you see order in all of creation as you reveal the magic of mathematics.
May you be surrounded by beauty as nature is revealed in art,
And art is revealed in nature.
And may you forever be in awe of this wonderful world
As you share the miracles of science.

May you be a beacon of light
As you spark the embers of interest
And fan a flame of enthusiasm
That bursts into a fire of passion
Which ignites a future
And transforms a young life forever.

A PRAYER OF THANKFULNESS FOR FRIENDSHIP

Thank you for a true friend,
    For the heart of another kind soul
        Connected to mine,
            Though time and space separates our bodies.
Thank you for those gentle spirits who lift me up
    And encourage me with loving words and deeds,
        Who have the ability to see the goodness in me
        And have the kindness to tell me.
Thank you for those ministering angels you place amongst us
    Who see me through your eyes,
        Who hear me through your ears,
            Who hold me with your arms,
                Who speak to me with your gentle words,
                    Who comfort my broken spirit with your Spirit.
Thank you for those divine beings sent from heaven's gates
    Who are filled with your presence,
        Who bring joy and peace and gentleness to my hurting heart,
            As they go about your work
                And become your hands and feet on earth.
Thank you for those heavenly messengers you send to me
    Who have your heart, Lord,
        Who love me with your love,
            And in doing so, heal me.
Of all your good gifts, O God,
    Perhaps none is so sweet
        As the precious gift of friendship.

A DOG'S BLESSING

A gentle smile, a gleeful wag,
A playful bark that says "hello."
A constant companion, a faithful friend,
My shadow wherever I go.

Unconditional love that knows no end,
You see only the best in me.
I wish that I could be as good
As the person that you see.

Trusting, patient, and understanding.
Always ready for a ride in the car.
I wish that I could be as good
As the dog you already are.

God bless you, my furry four-footed friend.
You are a treasure indeed.
For I found in you a blessing to my soul
When God gave you to me.

A FIREMAN'S BLESSING

God, bless this fireman,
Defender of our homes.
May you guide his every step
May he never walk alone.

Grant him courage, faith, and strength
That he needs for every fire.
Lift him up on eagle's wings
May he never falter, never tire.

Be the Protector of our protector,
Be the Shield of our shield.
Cover him with your hand of safety
From the dangers this life can yield.

May he see you, Lord, in every face
Of those he saves from harm:
In the face of the child and of the old man,
Of the mother and her babe in arms.

Grant us one more request, O Lord,
As they are called into the danger zone:
When the battle is over and won,
Grant that everyone goes home.

A PASTOR'S BLESSING

Bless this pastor, we pray, O Lord,
A shepherd of your flock.
Called to lead your sheep,
Called to be your living rock.

Give him a heart after yours, Father,
To lead others to Christ your Son.
May he hunger and thirst for you, Lord,
May he yearn for souls to be won.

Give him a mind after yours, Father,
To understand and know your ways.
Casting aside laws and putting on love,
May he humbly seek you and obey.

Give him leadership after yours, Father,
To lead by serving others,
Clothed in humility and cloaked in wisdom,
May he lead by loving another.

Give him words after yours, Father,
To bless and encourage those who hear.
Patient instruction, truth, and compassion,
May his words be your words we hold dear.

Give him strength after yours, Father,
To meet the race before him.
Courage and boldness and righteousness,
May he press on to defeat darkness afore him.

But most of all, give him love after yours, Father,
A love that knows no end,
To reach hurting, broken souls
So they see Jesus and call him "friend."

So shower your blessings upon our pastor
And upon his family, his circle of love.
For he is our gift from you, Lord,
A blessing sent from above.

A PHYSICIAN'S BLESSING

May the Spirit of the Great Physician
Fill you up and make you whole.
May his blood run through your instruments
And his song sing in your soul.

May his ancient wisdom
Be written on your heart.
May the timeless Oath of Hippocrates
Be your end and be your start.

May God's discernment be your guide,
May his skill run through your fingers.
May yours be the comforting hands of God,
May yours be his gentle voice that lingers.

May you see your patients through his eyes,
Each one a divine appointment.
May you treasure your sacred gift to heal
As the steward of a divine anointment.

May the mysteries of the body forever fill you with awe,
A living miracle that knows no end.
And know that where your science stops
Is where your faith begins.

May God use your healing hands
To restore and again make whole.
As you follow in the footsteps of the Great Healer
May you heal body, spirit, and soul.

A NURSE'S BLESSING

Father, bless this nurse,
Who with her hands so lovingly cares
For your children when they are weak
As we hold them in our prayers.

Bless her hands, O Lord,
To comfort those in need.
For her hands are your hands here on earth
In every action, in every deed.

Bless her feet, O Lord,
As they travel to and fro,
To spread healing and encouragement
To patients and loved ones in tow.

Bless her heart, O Lord,
One that is made for serving and giving,
A heart after yours, heavenly Father,
One that cherishes life and living.

Bless her sight, O Lord,
To see patients through your eyes,
Beloved children made in your image,
Precious in your sight.

Bless her hearing, O Lord,
To hear patients through your ears,
Your voice in every conversation,
Your hurt in every tear.

So rain down your blessings upon this nurse
And upon those whom she holds dear.
For she is your hands and feet on earth,
A blessing to all her patients here.

A BLESSING UPON MY FRIEND

May the Lord of all Good Gifts
Rain down his blessings upon you.
May the One who created the Universe
Inspire you to be all he created you to be.

May the Master Designer who designed you so wondrously
Encourage your beautiful heart and lift up your gentle soul.
May the Spirit of the Living God
Give your spirit wings to fly and joy to soar.

For you are a Blessing
To all who have the privilege of knowing you.
You are an Inspiration
To all whose paths intertwine with yours.

You are an Encouragement
With your gentle words and unending acts of kindness.
You are the Sunshine
Whose gracious spirit and warm smile illuminate a room.

Of all God's Good Gifts
Perhaps none is sweeter than Friendship.
How blessed I am
To call you Friend.

A BLESSING AS YOU GRADUATE

As you go forth from this day, may you be strong and bold.
May Christ's Spirit dwell within you as with the mighty saints of old.
As you embark upon your journey, as the road opens at your feet,
May the blessings of heaven be upon you as the course set before you, you complete.

May you be strong and courageous, may you banish all doubt and fear,
For the Lord your God is with you, whether you travel far or near.
May you seek first the Lord, may you give the Lord your best.
May he direct your paths and crown your efforts with success.

May Jehovah guide your passage and be a lamp unto your way.
May his Spirit be upon you and his Wisdom ever-present stay.
May Love, Joy, Peace, and Kindness be your guide.
May Patience, Gentleness, and Goodness protect you from foolish pride.

May you guard your affections, may you wisely entrust your heart.
May you choose your companions carefully, true friendship may you impart.
Fearfully and wonderfully God made you—a Masterpiece, a Treasure!
May you use your gifts in fulfilling work, may your joy be without measure.

May you wisely choose your path upon which the great saints have trod.
May you do Justice, may you love Mercy, and may you walk humbly with your God.

CANCER, ILLNESS, AND LIFE CHALLENGES

"Adversity introduces a man to himself."

Albert Einstein

Sometimes in life we get to stroll along on the mountaintops—on top of the world. Other times, we fight battles that are not of our choosing—whether cancer, a serious illness, financial difficulty, a job loss, or the breakdown of an important relationship. As a warrior is honed and sharpened through battles, the Lord uses adversity, painful as it may be, to hone us into being more God-like if we trust him to do so and lean into his Presence. The key is to decide to become better, not bitter, and to let God teach us through these trials.

In early 2013, I felt the Holy Spirit leading me to write a blessing for cancer patients. The very next week, Kelly, a dear college friend, informed our group of college buddies that she had been diagnosed with breast cancer and that she would soon be undergoing a double mastectomy. "The Battle Cry" seemed to be written just for her. I framed the blessing and brought it to her home, along with enough homemade dinners of my favorite comfort foods to feed an army for a month. I knew the Holy Spirit was using the words when she told me she read the blessing every day for encouragement. As I write this, she has just finished her last round of chemotherapy, and we are planning a girls' getaway weekend to celebrate the end of this battle.

I was once told that during the process of refining silver, the silversmith must heat the silver over a hot fire until the silver is liquid and its impurities are gone. The silversmith knows that the silver is pure and free of impurities when he can see his image in the molten silver. We all go through fiery trials from time to time. Some are consequences of our own failings, others are consequences of others' failings, and still others are simply part of the human experience. In all our trials, God promises that the testing of our faith develops perseverance, which is needed for us to be mature and complete in our faith (James 1:2–4). Rather than asking the Lord to take away our battles, like the saints who have gone before us, let us ask the Lord for courage and boldness to face the path set before us and gain victory over the enemy. And like the silversmith who sees the reflection of his face in the silver only when the silver is pure, may God see his reflection in us as we are purified and refined in our fires.

A PRAYER FOR BOLDNESS AND COURAGE

Fill me with your Spirit.
Love me with your love.
Give me boldness and courage
To face challenges undreamed of.

I'd like life to be easy.
I'd like life to be free.
But you are molding me to be like you,
Into the person I'm meant to be.

So fill me with fearlessness and faith
To meet the problems that I face.
Because you are building a new person
With your goodness and grace.

Fill me with your Spirit.
Love me with your love.
Equip me, transform me, refine me, redefine me,
So I'm like my Father above.

THE BATTLE CRY

Wondrously and wonderfully you are made:
A precious gift, a priceless treasure.
A beautiful spirit, a contagious smile,
Loveliness without measure.

You fight an unseen fight
In a battle you did not choose.
Expect a miracle! Banish fear and doubt!
For this battle you shall not lose!

You shall conquer the foe and defeat this enemy.
You shall finish as you have started:
Indomitable, Unbeatable, and Undefeatable,
Courageous and Lion-hearted!

Hope and Faith are on your side,
And Peace and Laughter and Love.
And Family and Friends to support and sustain
With God's healing hands from above.

May you arise better and stronger
When this battle is done.
A warrior honed and forged in the fire,
Victorious as the war is won!

BEREAVEMENT AND LOSS

❧

The human condition is a series of beginnings and losses. We are unable to move forward without leaving some things behind. In order to start something new, we must lose something old. In order for a sapling to grow into a mighty oak, a small acorn needs to dry up and fall to the ground. To see our children become independent adults, we must say good-bye to the sweet days of childhood when we were their hero. We must loosen our grip and give them permission to grow and go; we must give them wings to fly toward their own dreams. Likewise, as our parents and loved ones are called home to their Lord, we must say good-bye to those precious days when they were healthy and full of life.

We must loosen our grip and give them permission to go, and we must give them wings to fly toward the home of their true citizenship—heaven.

Loss can come in many forms – the death of a loved one, the breakdown of a marriage, the end of an important relationship, rejection and betrayal by friends and family members, the passing of a season of prosperity, the loss of a home or prized possessions through fire or theft or natural disaster, the loss of innocence through violence or abuse. We will not go through this world without loss. In fact, the Bible tells us there will be trials. God wants us to walk with him through our season of loss, to cry out our hearts to him, to let him heal our wounds with his love, and to trust that his plans and his ways are so much bigger and better than ours. During these times, let us crawl into the lap of Papa God, let him surround us with his warm and loving arms, allow him to comfort us with his warm soothing voice that we know so well, and just snuggle in his Presence until we are able to step out once again - holding his hand in ours.

My father was diagnosed with prostate cancer in 1998. He spent the last three months of his life in hospice, where he charmed the nurses, delighted the doctors, laughed, and continued to be thankful for even the smallest things in life. He not only taught us how to live; he taught us how to die. When the Lord called my father home in 2008, I was overcome with thankfulness for having been given such a wonderful father. Knowing that so few people have been blessed with a good father, I was filled with gratitude to have been blessed with a truly great one. My grief was overshadowed by my gratitude. My sadness at losing him was crowded out by joy in having had him at all! What a blessing! "A Prayer as Your Father Is Called Home" grew out of that experience.

As I write this, I have taken up residence in my mother's hospice room so that I can be with her as she stands at heaven's gate, waiting to be ushered in by the angels that surround us in this room. It has been a sweet time together as we wait for the Lord to call her home. A time that, I remind myself, few have the privilege of sharing with their parents. I have read to her from her and Dad's favorite book of poems. I sing the old hymns. I give her foot and hand and face massages. And I hold her hand during the day and throughout the night, so that she knows I am with her, even though she cannot respond. She has a peaceful, almost angelic, look on her face. If there are any furrowed brows, they soon disappear as I sing a hymn and gently stroke her head. With her servant's heart evident even now, the nurses comment on how gracious she has been, and how, until she could no longer speak, my mom would ask each morning what *she* could do for *them*. All the nurses want to know how, at ninety-four, she has such flawless skin and such a strong heart for someone who is waiting for her heavenly home. I tell them lots of homegrown vegetables, lots of hard work (she was still mowing her lawn well into her eighties), and lots of Jesus.

WAITING ON HEAVEN'S GATE

The hours creep on. I watch and I wait,
As you wait patiently for the opening of heaven's gate.

It is not yet your time, but the time is nigh
When you will see the Lord your God on high.

Then you will see Jesus face-to-face,
Surrounded by his glory, enfolded by his grace.

And he'll reach out his hand and say the words you long to hear:
"Well done, my daughter. Welcome home. We're glad you're here!"

And he'll show you around, you'll see old family and friends,
The same spirits with new bodies, from beginning to end.

Your heart will beat faster as you see Dad before you.
You've missed him for years; he loved and adored you.

"I've loved you in life. I've loved you forever.
Welcome home, Darling. We've a new life together."

But now you lie on this bed, and your eyes have grown dim,
And I pray that God gently and tenderly brings you to him.

And softly I hear the ruffling of angel's wings.
I look up and see these glorious things!

"Don't be afraid. She won't go alone.
We've come to get Jean and bring her home."

They did not linger, they did not wait,
But sweetly and gently, they brought her through heaven's gate.

A PRAYER AS YOUR FATHER IS WELCOMED HOME

May you rejoice in the knowledge
That your father was lovingly designed by his Creator,
That his life was planned by God
Since before the beginning of time.

May you delight in the fact
That he was uniquely and awesomely created
With a matchless combination of strengths and gifts and talents,
And wonderfully made in God's own image.

May you find comfort in the understanding
That with his every step, with his every journey,
The Lord went before him and behind him,
Placing his right hand on your father's shoulder to guide him.

May you know peace in the truth
That each day of his life on earth and each moment in eternity
Was ordained in the Lord's book and written by God's own hand
Before one of them came to be.

May you be encouraged by the vision
Of your father being welcomed by his Lord, saying,
"Well done, good and faithful servant!"
As angels rejoice in the homecoming of a child of the King.

May you celebrate the blessings of a wise and godly father,
Grateful that God chose him to be your dad, mentor, and unwavering supporter.
May your heart overflow with a thankfulness
That crowds out grief and despair.

May the One who placed the sun and the moon in the universe
And hung the stars up in the heavens
Calm your heart and still your soul
As he welcomes one of his beloved children home.

And may you live a life that continues your father's legacy of faith and good works,
A life that would make him proud to be your father,
A life that would bring him to say, "Well done, child after my own heart"
On that day when it is his turn to welcome you home.

GOOD-BYE TO A MOTHER

How do you say good-bye to a mother?
The person who gave you your very life.
The someone who, even before you were born,
Loved you more than life itself.

The sole individual, since the day you arrived,
Whose singular purpose was to do everything in her power
To provide you with love and security
And who, with her every breath,
Gave you wings to fly and a nest to return to
When you fell and needed to try again.

The only being on this earth
Who would have willingly sacrificed her life for yours,
And thought it a bargain at that.

Her undying passion was to make sure that her family loved the Lord
And made it home to the other side at the end of this life.

She prayed every night for you
And told you how much God loved you,
And she didn't stop telling you
Until you finally believed it for yourself.

She stayed up nights to rock you when you were a baby,
She stayed up nights to sew your second-grade school costume,
She stayed up nights when you turned sixteen and took out the car,
And when you finally grew up,
She still stayed up nights and stayed on her knees.

She was your biggest fan,
Your unwavering supporter,
And your closest confidante.

There is no one who walked the earth before her,
And there will be no one after,
Who has loved you as much
And with as much passion.

Of all the women in the world,
God especially chose her to be your mother,
To do his good works in her and through her,
And to mold you and shape you
Into the person he wanted you to be.

So I'm not sure how you say good-bye.

You have already said "thank you" to her
So many times for what she has done,
Even though it seems utterly inadequate.

Her kindness can never be repaid,
Nor would she want it to be.
You have lived your life
So that she would be proud of you—and she is—
And that's all she has ever asked of you.

You have cared for her in her old age
As she did for you when you were young.
And in doing so, have shown your deep respect for her,
Which is your duty and your privilege.
You have already thanked the Good Lord
For the blessing of having her in your life
And the legacy that she has left for generations.

But in the end,
When your mother goes home to be with her Lord—
Who has prepared a "welcome home" feast for her,
Who greets her with open arms and the words she has longed to hear:
"Welcome home, good and faithful servant!" —
There is little left to say except,
"Save room for me at your table, Mom. I'll be home soon."

And that, after all, is all she ever wanted.

A PRAYER AS YOUR SON IS WELCOMED HOME

May you rejoice in the knowledge that your son was lovingly designed by his Creator,
That his life was planned by God since before the beginning of time.

May you delight in the fact that he was wonderfully and wondrously created.
God chose the best of his father and the best of his mother,
And knit together in his mother's womb an exquisite gift
With a matchless combination of strengths and gifts and talents,
Magnificently made in God's own image.

May you find comfort in the understanding that with his every step,
With his every journey, the Lord went before him and behind him,
Placing his right hand on your son's shoulder to guide him.

May you know peace in the truth that each day of his life on earth
And each moment in eternity was ordained in the Lord's book
And written by God's own hand before one of them came to be.

May you be encouraged by the vision of your son being welcomed by his Lord,
"Well done, good and faithful servant!"
As angels rejoice in the homecoming of a child of the King.

May you be grateful that God chose you to be your son's parents, family, and role models:
"I, your heavenly Father, loved him first, and so I entrusted him to you."
May your heart overflow with a thankfulness that crowds out grief and despair.

And may the One who placed the sun by day and the moon by night
And hung the stars up in the heavens
Heal your heart, calm your spirit, and still your soul, trusting that
As much as you love your son, his heavenly Father loves him even more.

PRAYER OF A HURTING HEART

Lord, my heart hurts today.

I have entrusted my heart and my friendship.

I have given grace and endless patience,
    Not just in times of difficulty,
        But to people who are difficult.

And in return, my trust has been breached,
    My kindness has been answered with cruelty,
        My friendship has been rejected,
            My family has turned its back to me.

My heart is shattered,
    I can barely breathe,
        Life going forward will be sadly different.
        My hope is gone.

I am alone.

Yet your Word tells me you are with me,
    That your right hand guides me,
        Even though it is hard to feel your presence.

Your Word tells me to be strong and courageous
    And to banish doubt and fear,
        Even though doubt and fear is all I feel now.

Make your presence known to me,
    Fill me with your Holy Spirit,
        Replace my fears with strength,
            Replace my doubt with courage.

I do not ask you to take away this painful journey,
    But to give me boldness and steadfastness and safe passage,
        To open my ears to hear your voice,
            And to walk with me as a light in this darkness.

And when I have come through the valley,
    Lead me to the mountaintop,
        Stand with me on the summit,
            Give me back the joy and laughter that I once knew.

So that I may sing once more your praises,
    So that I may burst into song that overflows from a joyful heart,
        How great is my God!

A PRAYER WHEN YOU FEEL INSIGNIFICANT

Sometimes I feel so small, God.
I watch the news and see the political leaders of our time.
I read the papers and hear of the business titans of today.
I drive through neighborhoods with million-dollar houses.
And I wonder what you have called me to do.
    What am I here for?
        What plan do you have for me?
           Can you share it with me?

Your Word tells me that I am wondrously and wonderfully made.
Your Word tells me that I am made in your image, made to do your good works.
Your Word tells me that you have plans to prosper me.
And I wonder if I have chosen the right path.
    What gifts did you give me to use?
        Have I been a good steward of the opportunities you gave me?
          Does my life make any difference?

Your Son tells us to live on earth, but our home is in heaven.
Your Son gives us but one command: love God and love one another.
Your Son tells us to love, even those who are unlovely.
And I wonder if I have lived like my home is in heaven.
    Have I truly loved God with all my heart and soul and strength and mind?
        Have I loved others like God loves them?
          Have I loved even when love has been rejected?

Your Holy Spirit promises to fill us.
The Spirit speaks to us.
The Spirit fills us with your presence.

And I wonder some days why I don't feel it.
    Why do you feel so far away?
        Why can't I hear your voice?
            Why don't I sense your peace?

I feel small today, but I know that I serve a big God.
Tell me *your* plan,
    Show me *your* path for me,
        Teach me how to love like *you* do,
            Fill me with *your* presence,
                Open my ears to hear *you*,
                    Give me *your* peace.

YOU CARRIED ME

Lord, I ignored your whispers, those almost imperceptible tugs from Above.
I was overcome by the charm and deceptions, the false professions of "love."
"He is not a godly man, he is not the man I have chosen for you."
But I signed his contract on the eve of the wedding, and then I said "I do."

And since that day, you have carried me.

Through hundreds of threats to divorce, days after promising "only in death will we be parted,"
When I cried myself to sleep, after being used and discarded,
When he threatened to be with others if I could not satisfy,
Through the anger and the threats if I would not comply,

You carried me.

Through the dark night of abandon, through the bitter snow,
Thirty-five miles from the hell that I called home,
Dumped from his Mercedes, on that cold December eve,
As I shivered in my evening gown, through the gang-infested streets,

You carried me.

Through the eggshells on which I walked,
Through the anger when he talked,
Through the trips to the emergency room,
When I asked "Is this the man who was my groom?"

You carried me.

Through the movies, the websites, and the girls,
Who are eighteen, gorgeous, and bejeweled in pearls.
How can a mere wife compete?
Degraded and dehumanized, I was just a piece of meat.

You carried me.

When he said, "I don't care about you, I don't care what you think or what you feel,"
As he bragged of his Bible study attendance and the front pew in which he kneels.
Through the smiles and the laughter, when others think he's a jovial guy,
Behind the closed doors, when Dr. Jekyll turned into Mr. Hyde,

You carried me.

When I forgave and forgave, and then forgave again,
When I tried to be the gentle spirit and to be the light to men,
When my kindness was answered with evil and my pearls were trampled by swine,
You lovingly told me, "Daughter of the King, I love you, you are mine."

You carried me.

On the day I finally left, with my one small bag in the car,
I put on your armor, and though battered and scarred,
Through the pain and through the tears,
You loved me through the battle and gave me courage through my fears.

You carried me.

"That is not what I planned for you. I have planned so much more.
I will open up my riches in heaven. See, look what I have in store!
You are a gift, a treasure. I delight in you!
You are made to love and be loved, just like I love you.

"And I will carry you."

THE GIVERS AND THE TAKERS

Lord, thank you for your wisdom revealed to me:
"We cannot give what we do not have."

We who walk in the Spirit can give love and peace and kindness and joy
Only because your Spirit fills us with your fruit
And it overflows to others.

We are givers of your gifts,
Not earthly gifts.
We do not have, as humans, the power to give these,
Especially under the heat of battle from the Enemy.

But your Spirit in us can fill us
And allow us to give,
Even in the battle with the Enemy,
Or at least when the battle is over and you have won.

And so I beg, O Father,
That you fill me with your Presence,
So I can be a giver of goodness.

But those who do not walk in your Spirit
Have nothing inside of them to give.
They have none of your good gifts to give.
They cannot give.

But the Enemy distorts your good gifts.
And since the Enemy is in them,
That is all they can give—
A twisted, distorted version of your gift.

Instead of love,
    They give fear and control.
Instead of joy,
    They provide momentary entertainment.
Instead of peace,
    They provide temporary pause in the conflict
        Only when others agree to do things their way.
Instead of patience,
    They delay and defer.
Instead of kindness,
    They merely act in accordance with what will achieve their goals.
Instead of goodness,
    They put on an air of religion and attend church to impress others.
Instead of gentleness,
    They demand their own way.
Instead of faithfulness,
    They are not heart-connected to anyone,
        Their loyalty is only to themselves.
            They do not cherish or honor the gifts God has given them—
                Family, friends, honest work, a loving spouse—
                    These are only objects to serve them.
                        Deceit, affairs, illicit movies, and deviancy serve their
                      Sinful and selfish desires.
Instead of humbleness,
    They engage in self-aggrandizement,
        Entitlement,
            And putting others down to elevate themselves.
                Their hearts are too hard and full of pride,
                    To let God inside.

Instead of wisdom,
  They are fools—
    Unrepentant and unremorseful.
      Willing to give up God's good gifts
        For their stubbornness and hardened hearts.
Instead of self-control,
  They are quick to anger,
    Their rage overcomes them.
      They are unable and unwilling to do the right thing.
      God's way is not their way.

They are takers,
  They are empty inside,
    They must take from others to fill their empty souls.
    They cannot give what they do not have.

But those filled with your Spirit are givers.
  We seek to be full of your Presence.
    We give to others because you have filled us to overflowing.
      We give from the bounty of your gifts.
      You are the Giver, we are your vessels.

Lord, keep me in your Presence.
  May I never stray from your side.
    May your gifts overflow in me
      So that I may always share your gifts with others.

A HEART SONG OF LOVE—LOST AND FOUND

So many years have come and gone since we first met.
Are we still the same two people we once knew?
Are you still the kind and thoughtful man who stole my heart?
Am I still the same girl you adored with sparkling eyes of blue?

All these years, I've thought about you every day.
All these years, I've always wanted more.
The life we missed as I went off to college.
The hearts that broke as you went off to war.

Babies and houses and trips to foreign lands.
I have cried so many tears they were not with you.
You were searching and wishing and hoping you'd find me.
I was searching and wishing and hoping I'd find you.

My eyes had long lost their sparkle,
Replaced by sadness for a lost love that could never be.
War had taken its toll on you,
But you never stopped thinking of me.

Now that you've found me, our hearts are still attached.
Now that I've found you, it's sweeter than before.
The joys and struggles of life have honed us for the better.
Time apart has made me want us more.

We're in the autumn of our lives now,
So many wasted years that could have been.
Do we take a chance on love that never dies?
Do we take a chance on what always should have been?

I have loved you, Darling, forever.
I have loved you from the start.
Make a life with me, My Heart's Other Half.
I choose us, My Heart's Split-Apart.

NATURE AND THE SEASONS

"I love to think of nature as an unlimited broadcasting station,
through which God speaks to us every hour, if we only will tune in."
George Washington Carver

I truly love the four seasons. In genuine otter-like zest for life, I always think whichever season I am in is my favorite—until the next one comes. But perhaps spring holds the most joy for me when it arrives. Every year, after what I think must be 37 1/2 straight months of winter, spring finally comes to Chicago. The temperature peaks its way above 60 degrees or so in the last two weeks of April (although it could be as early as March or as late as June), and we are in the midst of a glorious renewal in spirit and in flora and fauna. The crab apple trees burst forth with white and pink and fuchsia snowballs, and the redbuds are in their glory with wispy twigs of purple. The scent of lilacs floats in and out of the air during an outdoor stroll.

In addition to the various and occasional smells of flowers, a deep breath during a walk outside produces that wonderful smell of spring—the perfect mixture of grass, black dirt, and earthworms. Whitetail deer appear on our front lawn in the mornings happily munching on breakfast salad greens. And the Canada geese couple, whom we have affectionately named Sam and Doris, take up residence in the nearby pond and give their budding family of little goslings swimming lessons as I drive by on Saturdays—with Sam in front, followed by their four children all in a row, and Doris bringing up the rear. Aunt and uncle geese, Bruce and Agnes, are close by on the bank of the pond cheering them on. Chippy, our home's resident chipmunk, makes his spring appearance and takes his position on the front stoop in his self-appointed role of announcer of the sunrise. And after months of silence, the backyard is once again filled with the swooping song of the cardinal.

I am in awe of the enormous variety of flowers that announce their arrival in every shape and size and color. I am humbled once again by the passage of Scripture reminding us that even King Solomon in all his glory was not clothed as beautifully as God has chosen to clothe the lilies. I am reminded that the Creator of the Universe must love variety, and I am thankful that he gave us such a beautiful world to be our playground.

I am also amazed as I realize anew that the spring is just what we need to lift our souls after a long winter. Human nature doesn't like change—we long for the familiar. But at the same time, we don't like to be in a rut, and we need variety from the humdrum of the everyday. And so the change of the seasons is the perfect solution for us mortal creatures: we get the variety we so desperately need, knowing that this spring, or summer, or fall, or winter—like all the springs and summers and falls and winters that have gone before it—will bring the familiar sounds and smells and beauty of ages past. I am grateful that the Master Designer has designed the seasons with us in mind.

SPRING

Thank you for the breath of springtime,
   The smell of fresh dirt,
      The warmth of a gentle breeze,
         As we breathe in new life and new love.

Thank you for waking up the earth from its slumber,
   Gently and tenderly, as she slowly releases the blanket of snow
      That has covered her during her long winter's nap.

Thank you for the symphony of sounds.
   The singsong of the robin,
      The chirping of the chipmunk,
         The soft background beat of the frogs,
            The screech of the red-winged blackbird,
               And the gentle coo of the mourning dove
                  All join together into an explosion of
                     Joyful music with no conductor, save you, Lord.

Thank you for the wardrobes of the flowers,
   Magnificent as they gently arise from their long repose
      And stretch their arms to the sun,
         Unfolding into a cacophony of colors and designs,
         Imagined in the mind only of you.
            Their beauty sings praise to you.

Thank you for the warmth of the sun,
     And the reds and blues and purples of the sunset,
          Each one painted by your own hands,
               Each one shouting your glory,
                    Each one a reminder of your endless love for us.

Thank you for our tall and gentle friends, the trees
     Who lift their arms toward heaven for nourishment
          While keeping firmly rooted in the rich dark soil.
               After a season of rest, they unfurl their leaves to give us oxygen to live,
                    To shade us from the sun and to protect us from the rain,
                         And to offer themselves as a living shelter and home
                              To their woodland companions, the squirrels and the birds.
                                   We can learn much from our friends, the trees.

Thank you, Lord for your promise of spring,
     of renewal,
          of rebirth,
               of new beginnings.

SUMMER

Thank you, God, for the summer,
  A season to play,
    A time to be fully alive,
      An age, however temporal, to marvel at the wonders of your world,
        A playground made by your hands for us to enjoy.

Thank you for making the life-giving waters:
  The magnificent oceans where the leviathan and whales frolic;
    The lazy lakes, home to the frogs and bass and little boys with fishing poles;
      The mighty rivers to carry us and our cargo;
        The waterfalls that fill us with awe and wonder;
          The crisp mountain streams tripping over boulders and stones
            As they bring the melting snow from the crests to the valleys.

Thank you for creating the creatures of the air:
  The majestic eagle, lord of the skies;
    The melodious songbirds, troubadours of the trees;
      The graceful dragonflies, woodland fairies on diaphanous wings of the wind;
        The breathtaking butterflies, delicate beauties of the breezes;
          The fireflies, lights of wonder on a summer night;
            And the hardworking honeybees, caretakers of the flowers.

Thank you for molding the regal mountains, as clay in the potter's hands:
  The snowy peaks reaching heavenward, majestic and rugged;
    The blue smoky haze of your breath hovering over the Ancient Ones, soft and rolling;
      The great monoliths, like mere pebbles to you;
        And the friendly hills, grass-covered for the cattle to roam.

Thank you for spreading out your hands and waving the plains into being:
> For fields of wheat and corn and beans, as far as the eye can see;
>> For ranches of cattle, and for cowboys who live by a code;
>>> For wide expanses and wild mustangs;
>>>> And for making them both beautiful and bold.
>>>>> Thank you for feeding us, body and soul, with the fruit of the flatlands.

Thank you for designing the wonders of the world:
> For drawing a line in the desert with your finger,
>> To show off your red and orange masterpiece we call the Grand Canyon;
>>> For setting the bowels of the earth to boil and overflow
>>>> To remind us of your faithfulness in Old Faithful;
>>>>> For creating the most beautiful of temples I have been permitted to enter,
>>>>>> Your cathedral at Yosemite;
>>>>>>> For pulling back the curtain to show your reflection
>>>>>>>> In the Northern Lights.

Thank you for creating the creatures of the land and sea,
> Magnificent in all their wondrous diversity:
>> From the trumpet of the elephant and the roar of the lion,
>>> To our friends the dolphins and the curious platypus;
>>>> From the slithering snakes and the lumbering tortoise,
>>>>> To the giant whales and ethereal jellyfish;
>>>>>> I marvel at your imagination and craftsmanship.
>>>>>> All of creation shouts praises to your artistry.

Lord, in this season, may I see you in the works of your hands;
> May I be brought to my knees at the sight of your mountains and plains and seas,
>> May my soul be filled with your Spirit and drenched in the rain of your blessings,
>> May the beauty of your earth stir me to worship a God so, so big,
>>> And may I forever be in awe of you and the wonders you have made.

AUTUMN

Thank you, Lord, for this season of autumn,
> When you pull your red and orange and yellow curtains around summer
>> As it gently draws to a close,
>>> And the earth takes a deep breath as it rests from its busyness
>>>> In preparation for the serene and silent winter.

Thank you for your brilliant tapestry woven into the fabric of the hillsides and highways:
> Of sugar maples, resplendent in their tangerines and peaches;
>> Of the viburnum and sumac, spreading their blazing crimson across the floor of the forest;
>>> Of the elegant mountain aspen and birch, radiant as their gilded leaves reach heavenward;
>>>> Of the noble oaks, understated and subdued in hues of auburn and mahogany;
>>>>> A kaleidoscope of colors created in your art studio of earth.

Thank you for the harvest and the fruit of the land:
> For the golden wheat—the staff of the bread of life;
>> For the tall corn and the lowly beans—sustainers of the world;
>>> For the apples and pears—nature's sweet delights;
>>>> For the acorns and nuts—food to the frolicking squirrels;
>>>>> For the pumpkins and squash—warm traditions of the feast giving thanks.

Thank you for the creatures of the land:
> The cattle of the plains;
>> The pigs of the barnyard;
>>> The geese of the sky;
>>>> The sheep of the mountain;
>>>>> The deer of the forest;
>>>>>> The fish of the streams.
>>>>>>> We humbly take these spirits,
>>>>>>>> Made by you so that we might live.

Thank you for the season of giving thanks:
　　For opening the doors of heaven
　　　　And raining your blessings upon us;
　　　　　　For peace and shelter amidst the storms;
　　　　　　　　For families who give us a glimpse of heaven;
　　　　　　　　For friends who share our joys and sorrows;
　　　　　　　　For cherished ones whom we cherish;
　　　　　　　　　　For loved ones who share their love with us,
　　　　　　　　　　Even when we are unlovely.

Lord, awaken our memories.
　　Remind us in this season
　　　To be thankful:
　　　　To be mindful of your blessings falling on us like warm gentle rain;
　　　　　To slow from our busyness;
　　　　　　To treasure those we treasure;
　　　　　　To love extravagantly;
　　　　　　　To be surrounded by your presence.

WINTER

Thank you, Lord, for this season of winter,
    To rest and renew,
        To nest and review,
            To snuggle in front of the fire,
                To gather around warm bowls of soup,
                To take time to read.

Thank you for the snow.
    You make each snowflake unique,
        Just like you make each one of us unique.
            Thank you for the quiet that envelops the earth
                And the clocks that stop their endless work
                    As you send your snowflakes silently from heaven
                    To softly blanket the ground.

Thank you for the ice,
    Glistening silvery fingers painted on the naked trees,
        Radiant in the cold sunlight
            The morning after an ice storm—
                Your every brushstroke a work of art,
                    Each flourish of the palette knife a painting,
                        Each evergreen and oak a topiary sculpture.
                          Together, a magnificent masterpiece of white.

Thank you for the cold
    To slow the earth,
        To hibernate, to sleep, to rest,
            To lie dormant in anticipation of spring,
                To wait unhurried and silent before life bursts forth again.

Lord, help me use this season to be unrushed,
To seek you in the pages of your Book,
To find you in our quiet times together,
To hear your gentle voice as it echoes in my spirit,
To be still and to feel your presence.

GOD'S CATHEDRAL

How perfect the handiwork of God!

What monument could mere man build
 That could come close to rivaling
  The marvelous temple of worship he created?

The stately pines reach to the heavens
 Forming a canopy above
  And a quiet sanctuary below,
   Surrounded by their ancient, solemn columns.

The wind through the boughs
 Is a gentle choir
  Whispering to our souls of his great love for us.

The loon, with her sorrowful song,
 The chipmunks and all their chattering,
  The cry of the lone hawk,
   With the chorus of a thousand frogs
    Blend in perfect harmony
     As God's chosen soloists.

The autumn colors of crimson, rust, and gold
 Against the white birch bark
  Paint an unsurpassed palette of stained glass.

Pine needles and moss form a soft, velvety verdant carpet;
 The aromas of the fir trees blend into a most intoxicating incense.

The pristine lake sparking with a million diamonds
    Is God's holy water,
        Sanctified and sent from heaven
            During his own magnificent thunderstorm and fireworks show
                Proclaiming his majesty with resounding trumpets and cymbals.

The berries in all their colors
    Are the fragrant host of the Eucharist;
        The streams and rivers,
            The sweet wine of Communion.
                How can we eat and drink of his good earth
                    But in remembrance of our Lord who made it?

How majestic are the mountains
    And the great monoliths
        Draped in purple and topped with white snow
            Forming the stone edifice of God's House of Worship.

The blue of the skies and the stars in the heavens
    Are the celestial ceilings of the Lord's basilica.

The baby in my belly wriggles and squirms like a child in a pew,
    Another of his miracles,
        Waiting impatiently to announce to the world
            That another child of the King has arrived!

Not in the history of man have we ever, nor shall we ever,

Construct any edifice of worship,

Any house of prayer,

Any temple,

Any church,

As glorious as the Holy Cathedral he created for himself
And for us to enjoy.

I stand in awestruck wonder of his creation and glory.

YOUR LOVE IS EVERYWHERE

You hung the stars up in the sky.
You make the newborn baby cry.
They say you came, you lived, you died.
I ask you, What's the reason? Why?

You made the grass so sweet and clean.
You made the hues from blue to green
And all the colors in between.
But you ask me to believe in you—sight unseen.

You made the shadows on the crystal white moon.
You taught the birds and the lovers to croon.
You composed the sweet, sad song of the loon.
Must I really believe in you so soon?

You send the rainbow after the rain,
A promise not to flood the world again.
You make us all different—some pretty, some plain.
Did you really die and rise again?

They say a relationship with me you've planned—
To love me and hold me in your hand,
To walk with me and with me stand.
This is hard for me to understand.

But I'm beginning to see it now more clearly.
Perhaps, like a father, you loved me so dearly
That you came down as one of us—or quite nearly
So we could love you more sincerely.

And perhaps, just perhaps, you loved me so
That you made this beautiful world so I would know
That you made it for me, to live in and grow.
And with its beauty, your love for me to show.

The mountains and the sunsets and the meadows so fair,
The flowers and trees and clouds floating here and there,
They burst forth with your love, and in awe I simply stare.
You are not unseen—your love is everywhere!

EVERYDAY PRAYERS

I love that God wants a relationship with us just like an earthy father wants a relationship with his children. Like any good relationship with an earthly father, a warm, close relationship with our heavenly Father takes time and effort—time set aside to talk with each other, time to listen to each other, time spent writing and reading letters from each other, and time to do the things together that the other enjoys. God would love to hear from us every day, just as he talks to us every day. Not just for a minute or two, or only when we are in trouble; he really wants us to share our hearts. He listens intently to everything we have to tell him as if we were his only child and he had nothing else in the world to do other than listen to us. And he would love us to put down our cell phones, televisions, computers, and busy schedules for a few moments and just be still so that we can hear his voice and listen to him as he shares his heart with us.

Fortunately, there is no magic language that we need to use to talk to God. When I read the psalms of David, I'm struck by how he just pours out whatever is on his heart to his dad. Sometimes he is in tears, sometimes afraid, sometimes joyful—and our heavenly dad wants to hear it all.

One of my favorite prayers is the Breastplate of St. Patrick, a wonderful prayer by the fourth-century patron saint of Ireland. A breastplate, of course, is a piece of armor that defends the heart and body against the blows of the enemy. It is the forerunner to the modern day flak jacket. The "breastplate of righteousness" is one of the pieces of spiritual armor that we need to put on to defend ourselves against the attacks of Satan (Ephesians 6:10–17). I suspect that St. Patrick "put on" his breastplate of prayer every morning as he committed to bind himself to God.

The dictionary tells us that *bind* means to fasten or secure with a tight band or bond. In the world of chemistry, chemical binding is the process in which atoms or molecules become intertwined so that their prior individual characteristics no longer exist, replaced by the new characteristics of the new substance.

When hydrogen and oxygen are bound together as H_2O, neither the characteristics of hydrogen nor the characteristics of oxygen continue to exist, but instead, the new substance, water, has completely different characteristics.

I like to think that when God gets hold of us, when we bind ourselves to him, we become a new substance with a new character, and therefore we possess new characteristics that are different from our old ones. I particularly like the part of the prayer in which St. Patrick asks Christ to be all around him. Imagine going through your day binding yourself to God and surrounded by Jesus on all sides! This vision of Christ surrounding us throughout our day, taken from St. Patrick, is the inspiration for my "Morning Prayer."

THE BREASTPLATE OF ST. PATRICK

I bind unto myself today
The strong Name of the Trinity,
By invocation of the same,
The Three in One and One in Three.

I bind this day to me for ever
By power of faith, Christ's incarnation;
His baptism in the Jordan River;
His death on the Cross for my salvation;
His bursting from the spicèd tomb;
His riding up the heavenly way;
His coming at the day of doom;
I bind unto myself today.

I bind unto myself the power
Of the great love of the cherubim;
The sweet "well done" in judgment hour,
The service of the seraphim,
Confessors' faith, Apostles' word,
The Patriarchs' prayers, the Prophets' scrolls,
All good deeds done unto the Lord,
And purity of virgin souls.

I bind unto myself today
The virtues of the starlit heaven,
The glorious sun's life-giving ray,
The whiteness of the moon at even,
The flashing of the lightning free,

The whirling wind's tempestuous shocks,
The stable earth, the deep salt sea,
Around the old eternal rocks.

I bind unto myself today
The power of God to hold and lead,
His eye to watch, his might to stay,
His ear to hearken to my need.
The wisdom of my God to teach,
His hand to guide, his shield to ward,
The word of God to give me speech,
His heavenly host to be my guard.

Against the demon snares of sin,
The vice that gives temptation force,
The natural lusts that war within,
The hostile men that mar my course;
Or few or many, far or nigh,
In every place and in all hours,
Against their fierce hostility,
I bind to me these holy powers.

Against all Satan's spells and wiles,
Against false words of heresy,
Against the knowledge that defiles,
Against the heart's idolatry,
Against the wizard's evil craft,
Against the death wound and the burning,
The choking wave and the poisoned shaft,
Protect me, Christ, till thy returning.

Christ be with me, Christ within me,
Christ behind me, Christ before me,
Christ beside me, Christ to win me,
Christ to comfort and restore me.
Christ beneath me, Christ above me,
Christ in quiet, Christ in danger,
Christ in hearts of all that love me,
Christ in mouth of friend and stranger.

I bind unto myself the Name,
The strong Name of the Trinity;
By invocation of the same.
The Three in One, and One in Three,
Of whom all nature hath creation,
Eternal Father, Spirit, Word:
Praise to the Lord of my salvation,
Salvation is of Christ the Lord.

—Traditional, translation by Cecil F. Alexander

A MORNING PRAYER

Good morning, Lord!

Father, Son, and Holy Spirit,
Blessed Trinity;
Your still small voice—today may I hear it,
May I live in light of eternity.

Be with me today, Lord,
As I bind myself to you.
May your Word be my sword,
Surround me with you.

Christ, be with me and within me.
Go behind me and before me.
Walk beside me and win me,
Comfort me and restore me.

Christ, go beneath me and above me.
Be with me in quiet and in danger.
Reign in the hearts of those who love me.
Love be in the words of friend and stranger.

Good morning, Lord!

I know you are with me today,
As you bind yourself to me—
Guiding my path, lighting my way,
Surrounding me with the Trinity.

A PRAYER AT DINNER

Heavenly Father,

    We thank you for this food.

        We thank you that when you were creating the earth, and all the diversity in it,

           you created food for us

                to eat to nourish our bodies,

                    to gather around tables to nourish our souls,

                    to taste good to bring us pleasure,

                        and in endless selections to satisfy our need for variety.

We thank you for this home.

    We thank you for the shelter it brings from the storms outside to warm our bodies.

      And we thank you for the shelter it brings from the storms of life to warm our hearts.

We thank you for the people gathered around this table.

    We thank you that in your grand design,

        you chose us to be together

        and made us a family.

Thank you for the unique way that you wove each one of us while we were yet unborn.

    And, in your love, gave each of us as a gift to each other.

      May we hold dear the magnificent tapestry of our family.

      May we forever cherish each other as your precious treasures.

We thank you for your love.

Shape us into your image.

    Give us hearts to love like you,

        eyes to see others like you,

           ears to hear your voice,

                voices to speak your words,

                    and fingers and toes to be your hands and feet to those in need.

    Amen

A HEART SONG OF THE SPIRIT

Let your grace rain on me, let your grace rain down on me.
Let your grace heal my hurting soul. Let your grace rain down on me.

Let your joy rain on me, let your joy rain down on me.
Let your joy fill my sad soul. Let your joy rain down on me.

Let your peace rain on me, let your peace rain down on me.
Let your peace calm my troubled soul. Let your peace rain down on me.

Let your patience rain on me, let your patience rain down on me.
Let your patience slow my busy soul. Let your patience rain down on me.

Let your kindness rain on me, let your kindness rain down on me.
Let your kindness flood my wretched soul. Let your kindness rain down on me.

Let your goodness rain on me, let your goodness rain down on me.
Let your goodness transform my selfish soul. Let your goodness rain down on me.

Let your faithfulness rain on me, let your faithfulness rain down on me.
Let your faithfulness keep my wandering soul. Let your faithfulness rain down on me.

Let your gentleness rain on me, let your gentleness rain down on me.
Let your gentleness soften my hardened soul. Let your gentleness rain down on me.

Let your self-control rain on me, let your self-control rain down on me.
Let your self-control soothe my angry soul. Let your self-control rain down on me.

For it's your Spirit that I need. I need your Spirit to make me whole.
Spirit of the Living God, fill me up and make me whole, fill me up and fill my soul.

Let your love rain on me, let your love rain down on me.
Let your love fill this needy soul. Let your love rain down on me.

A BLESSING OF PSALM 139

May the Lord lay his hand upon you.
>May he surround you with his loving kindness,
And walk before you to guide you
>And behind you to protect you.

May his Spirit be with you wherever you may go!

If you climb the mountains to the heavens,
>May you find him there.
If you dive to the depths of the sea,
>May you sense his presence with you.

If you rise in the morning on the wings of the dawn
>Or return in the evening on the far side of the sea,
Even there, may his right hand guide you
>And hold you close to him.

May you rest in the knowledge
>That God planned you before the universe was formed.
May you find joy in the promise
>That you are wondrously and wonderfully created.

May you rejoice in the assurance
>That you were made by God's own hand in his image.
May you cling to his covenant
>That our Father abides in you and you in him.

And may his peace be upon you,
    Knowing that all your days have been ordained,
That each of your moments was written in his Book of Life,
    Before even one of them came to be.

A BLESSING OF FAITH, HOPE, AND LOVE

May you be blessed with a Faith that is steadfast and bold,
And may God bless you with the Faith of the mighty saints of old.
May your doubting be small and your Faith be courageous,
May your Faith be your foundation, may it be your Rock of Ages.

May you Believe in things unseen, and Hope in things to come,
May your trust rest in the Lord and the wonderful things he has done.
May you know God's quiet voice, may he touch your heart anew,
May you be still and listen when he whispers to you.

May you know the Love of family and feel the Warmth of friends
And find Comfort in a God so big that his Love never ends.
May your heart be full and joyous, and your cup be overflowing,
May Love reign in your life, may it be ever-growing.

I wish you Faith and Hope and Love
And all the blessings that they bring,
But most of all I wish you Love, the greatest of all things.

THE GIFT

Two thousand years ago, God did not send us a politician—
because we did not need another political leader.

He did not send us a statesman—
because we did not need another diplomat.

He did not send us a scientist—
because we did not need more scientific advancements.

He did not send us a physician—
because we did not need more medical care.

He did not send us an information technology specialist—
because we needed neither more information nor more technology.

He did not send us an economist—
because we did not need more money.

He did not send us a lawyer—
because we did not need more laws.

He did not send us a musician—
because we did not need to be entertained.

Two thousand years ago, God sent us Jesus—
because then, as now, we needed Love.

A PRAYER OF PEACE

Breath of Heaven,
Precious Gift from Above,
Bring to us your Peace on Earth,
Goodwill to Men, and Love.

May I be your hands
To serve those in need,
May I be your feet
To spread the Gospel of Peace.

May I be your arms
To hug a hurting soul,
May my heart beat as yours
To love and make us whole.

May I see through your eyes
As a loving Father sees,
May I hear with your ears
Sounds of your children at your knees.

May I walk with you daily,
Touch my heart and make me see.
May I be still and listen
When you whisper to me.

Light of the World, Prince of Peace,
Gift from God's own Hands,
Use me to spread goodwill to men
And love and peace through all the lands.

SIMPLE BLESSINGS

May the God who placed the stars in the heavens
And hung the moon above the earth
Place a firm foundation under your feet
And angelshine in your home.

May the One who stilled the waters with his hand
And calmed the seas with his voice
Bring peace to your heart
In a tumultuous world.

May Yahweh, who clothes the lilies in all their splendor
And dresses the sunset in robes of brilliance,
Provide warm clothing in a cold winter
And beauty to stir your soul.

May El Shaddai, who sent manna from heaven
And birds from the sky,
Provide a feast for your table
And laughter to lift your spirit.

May the Creator of Life
And the Author of Love
Bless you with love in your life
And life in your love.

And may your life be such that
Your heart and your treasures
Are not kept precariously here on earth,
But rather are entrusted safely with your Lord in heaven.

BLESSINGS OF THE SPIRIT

May you have Love in your heart and home,
May Joy be in your soul.
May Peace be yours, indeed, Shalom,
May Patience make you whole.

May Kindness be in your every word
And Goodness in every deed.
May you be Gentle and Self-Controlled,
May Faithfulness be your creed.

May the Fruit of the Spirit dwell richly in you
So that others can surely say
That the wealth of a life is not measured in gold,
But in lives one touches along the way.

May you hear God's voice within your soul,
The still, soft whisper from Above.
May you walk with God on this journey of life
Surrounded by his Love.

FILL ME WITH YOUR SPIRIT

Fill me with your Spirit, Lord.
Love me with your love.
Infuse me with your Presence,
Great Heavenly Father above.

Let me love the way that you do.
Let me give instead of take.
Let others see Jesus instead of me.
Let me follow you and all other things forsake.

Let me bring your Joy to those around me.
Let your Peace be upon me as I am still.
Let your Patience calm my spirit.
Let your Will be my will.

Let your Kindness flow through me.
Let your Goodness be in all I do.
Let your Faithfulness be ever present in me.
Let your Light in me shine through.

Let your Gentleness soften my hard edges.
Let your Self-Control be my guide.
Let your Wisdom guide my steps.
Let your Spirit in me abide.

Envelop me with your Presence.
Let my heart be your dwelling place.
Take my life and let it be the canvas
Upon which you paint your amazing grace.

Let me see myself as cherished.
Not for what I can do or be.
But because I am your treasure
And because of your marvelous love for me.

SONGS OF THE HOLY LAND

❧

When I am outside in God's cathedral, I am often overwhelmed by the beauty of the earth that he made—so much so that I burst into song. Usually "How Great Thou Art" or "Amazing Grace." I just can't help myself. I am reminded of the words of Jesus when the disciples shouted joyful praises as he arrived in Jerusalem and the Pharisees told them to keep quiet; Jesus responded that if the people were quiet, the very stones would cry out. If I don't sing, the stones (and trees and plants and mountains!) would burst forth in praise! All of creation sings of God's glory.

So when I had the special privilege of visiting the Holy Land, the weight of the importance of the miracles that God did there were impressed upon me. As I trod on the same stones that Jesus and the disciples traveled, and touched the same tomb that Jesus was buried in, the Holy Spirit washed over me. I was both humbled and in awe of the extent of God's love for us and the lengths that he will go to bring us back to him. The words of Scripture seemed to jump off the pages, and the ancient stories that I had read so many times became alive and real and *now* as I walked the desert where Moses walked and sailed the sea where Jesus sailed. The songs I include here are two that God put on my heart during my time in Israel and Egypt.

SONG ON THE SHORE OF THE SEA OF GALILEE

The God who put the Universe in place,
The One who invented time and space,
The One who formed the earth and made it spin,
Is the One in my heart who lives within.

The One who set the stars up in the sky
Gave us the sun by day, the moon by night.
The One who came to earth to show the way
Is the One who walks beside me day by day.

He made the sea—and walked with us.
In Galilee—he talked with us.
In Jerusalem—he bled and died
So we may have life.

The God who made the mountains and the sea,
The One who so loved you and me,
Who was born in Bethlehem under a star above,
I can't believe loves even me . . . what love.

THE SONG OF MOUNT SINAI

In this place, we have seen your majesty.
In this place, your handiwork we see.
You spread your hand across the land.
You dipped your fingers in the sea.
In this place, it's all so overwhelming to me.

In this place, we have seen your faithfulness.
In this place, we're overcome by gratefulness.
You led your people through the sand
And guided them with your loving hand.
In this place, it's now so real to me.

In this place, we feel your presence near.
In this place, although the Dark One lives here,
You've chosen us to take a stand
To be a light within this land.
In this place, I feel you near to me.

We see your mighty wonders.
We know of your miracles done.
We hear your children sing praises
That you're the Truth and Only One.
And we can feel your Spirit moving in this place.

BLESSINGS FOR THE
SPECIAL YOUNG PEOPLE IN MY LIFE

❧

I wrote my first blessing many years ago for dear friends who were getting married. Soon afterward, babies started to arrive, and as we all know, new babies and new parents need extra blessings from God. As I thought of the blessings I wanted to give, I researched the meaning and history of the names that were bestowed on each child, and I contemplated how their young lives might unfold.

Throughout Scripture, one's name was very important. Names were carefully chosen. In ancient times, a name described the attributes of a person, and it often foretold a person's life trajectory. I wondered

177

how the names of these precious gifts would influence their lives. I pondered what special gifts God had given them that we had yet to discover, and imagined how their young lives would leave a mark on this world.

I love the promises of Psalm 139 that God created each one of us wonderfully and wondrously, that our heavenly Father had a plan for us before we were even conceived, and that the Lord ordained each of our days before even one came to be. I find peace and comfort in knowing that God called the psalm writer David "a man after my own heart" and that we, too, can be called his friends if we earnestly seek him. And as I looked upon these wee ones, so fresh from the hands of God, I marveled at his work and wondered how he had uniquely equipped and gifted them to bring glory to himself and bring his king-dom here on earth.

The prophet Micah asked what the Lord requires of us—and the Lord responded, "To act justly and to love mercy and to walk humbly with your God" (Micah 6:8). And so I hoped, above all things, that these little ones would walk with the Lord all their days and that he would call them "friend" and "one after my own heart."

As I asked the Lord's blessings on these little ones, I asked that my words would be his words—that not only would these words be an encouragement, but also that they would inspire their recipients to draw close to God and to embody the virtues of their names. Into each blessing, I wove in the meanings of their names or the attributes of their namesakes, and I asked God to bless them as he blessed the saints of old. In each blessing, I prayed that they would come to know the Lord and walk with him on this journey called life.

In time, the Spirit led me to write blessings for my children, Donny, Christy, and Marty; godchil-dren, Dan, Tiana, and Jordan; and other dear young ones as they reached milestones in their lives. I mounted the blessings and set them in beautiful frames. As I wrote each one, I rewound the videotape of their lives in my mind, remembering precious moments. In particular, when my daughter Christy asked to be baptized, I remembered her solo adventure to the park when she was only two. Born with an abundance of confidence, she and her beloved stuffed Baby Raccoon decided to go on a summer jaunt without telling Mom. After nearly two hours of a missing child, my prayers for her safety had never been so fervent, and I have never been so grateful for answered prayer! Her name, Christina, means "Christ bearer." It was then that I realized her boldness sprang from the saints and apostles—the Christ bearers of old—who boldly proclaimed Christ. In a quiet conversation with God one evening, he informed me that Christy's boldness and confidence was one of God's gifts to her, with which she will blaze a trail and accomplish amazing things. My first born is Donald, which means "leader." As he has grown into adulthood, it has been a joy to watch his natural leadership skills develop. And the caboose is Marty, who, even at an early age, seemed to walk in the footsteps of Martin Luther.

Soon my children's friends asked for their own blessings from "Mama K," as they called me, to commemorate special occasions in their lives, and so I kept writing—and I kept asking God that my words would be his words. Now, rather than the normal gifts that are soon discarded or forgotten, I usually give the gift of a personal framed blessing for new babies and special occasions. The first babies I started writing blessings for are now almost in their preteen years, and many of my children's friends are in college. Whenever I see them, they let me know that their blessings have a special place of honor on their bedroom dressers. And that tells me that God is still imprinting his mark on their hearts, the Spirit is still using his words to move in their lives, and that, every day when they see their blessings, the Lord reminds them that his blessings to them are new every morning.

A BLESSING UPON DONNY
ON THE DAY OF YOUR TWENTY-FIRST BIRTHDAY

Your name means "leader," may you be strong and bold.
May you lead by God's own hand, as the great leaders of old.

May you have the faith of Moses from which you never depart.
When you stand on the shores of your Red Sea, may God make your seas part.
May your courage be that of Joshua, may you be strong and courageous.
May your life leave a legacy and speak to generations throughout the ages.

May your wisdom be as Solomon's, a guiding light in your life,
A source of wealth and prosperity, a beacon in times of strife.
May your heart beat as David's, with humbleness, poetry, and art,
May you seek God, and may he call you "A man after my own heart."

May your leadership be that of Jesus, unlike all the rest,
May God's Spirit dwell deep within you and beat within your breast.
May he light a fire within you, and may you keep bright the flame,
Of the faith and hope and love that you find in Christ's name.

May your godly wisdom and kindness grow and joyfulness resound.
Your good heart and thoughtful ways—may they always abound.
May you always be thankful, may you give the Lord your best,
May the gifts of a wife and children be with you, may you be forever blessed.

You have been my firstborn, a special gift from above
Entrusted to me for a short time, now I give you back with love.
I pray a mother's enduring prayer, I ask the Lord only this:
That God would be on your side, and that you might always be on his.

And now, may you always walk with Jesus, may your journey never end,
May you call him "Lord," and may he always call you "Friend."

A BLESSING UPON CHRISTINA
ON THE DAY OF YOUR BAPTISM

I made a promise to God when you were just two.
You had run off to the park a mile away and we could not find you.
"I will dedicate her life so that she will always know thee,
If you just bring her back safely, wherever she may be."

Your name means "Christ bearer." May you be strong and bold.
May your life be dedicated as Christ's bearers of old.
May you keep strong the faith and keep bright the flame.
May Christ's love be imprinted upon you as you bear his name.

May you keep your childlike wonder of a God so, so big.
May you recognize his handiwork in every rock and twig.
May you stand in awesome wonder when you hear a newborn baby cry.
May you tremble at God's majesty when you feel the thunder and watch the sky.

May you grow to be beautiful, wise, and courageous.
May your life leave a legacy in the history pages.
May the Spirit of God dwell richly in you.
May you seek the Lord's guidance in all that you do.

May you always be thankful, may you seek to know truth.
May you know Jesus as Savior from the days of your youth.
May you know God's voice, may he touch your heart anew.
May you be still and listen when he whispers to you.

May kindness and generosity be the fabric of your soul.
In you may the Master Weaver weave a tapestry lovely to behold.
May he use your hands as his to give to those in need,
And use your feet to spread his love and give you Godspeed.

May your life bear Christ always, may he be engraved upon your heart.
May your soul sing out in worship, "My God, how great thou art!"
And when you come to the end of your journey, when from this world you depart,
May the Lord say, "Welcome home, Christ bearer, one after my own heart."

A BLESSING UPON MARTIN
ON THE DAY OF YOUR BAPTISM

Your name runs through the ages, may you be strong and bold.
May your faith be steadfast and courageous, as Martin Luther of old.
Today you make a stand for Christ in front of many others.
"Here I stand," proclaims Martin. "I can do no other."

Your heart beats to a different drummer, unlike all the rest,
May God's Spirit dwell deep within you and beat within your breast.
May he light a fire within you, and may you keep bright the flame,
Of the faith and hope and love that you find in Christ's name.

May your godly wisdom and kindness grow and joyfulness resound.
Your tender heart and thoughtful ways—may they always abound.
May you always be thankful, may you give the Lord your best,
May you always be the peacemaker, may you be forever blessed.

May the belt of truth encircle your waist
And the breastplate of righteousness be firmly in place.
May your feet be swift to spread the gospel of peace,
May you pray in the Spirit, may your prayers never cease.

May your faith be strong, may it be your steadfast shield
And grant you victory over all the storms that life can wield.
May you don the helmet of God's sweet salvation,
May it protect you from harm and all of life's temptations.

May your only weapon be your two-edged sword
Of his Spirit within you, of the Word of the Lord.
May you be clothed head to toe with Jesus' great love,
May God pour down his blessings from heaven above.

May God use you as his vessel, may your soul be his dwelling place,
May your life be a canvas upon which God paints his amazing grace.
May you walk in righteousness where saints and angels have trod,
May you declare from the mountains, "A mighty fortress is our God!"

May you talk with God daily, may he touch your heart anew,
May you be still and listen when he whispers to you.
May you walk with Jesus and follow his ways,
May he bless you and call you friend all of your days.

And when you come to the end of your journey, when from this world you depart,
May the Lord welcome you home and call you "Marty, a man after my own heart."

MADISON'S LULLABY

Madison, fresh from the hand of God,
Madison, you came from where angels have trod,
Madison, a daughter of the King,
Just for you, he's given everything.

You are made by him so wonderfully,
You are handpicked for this family,
You are welcomed here so happily,
You are made by him so lovely.
Yes you are.

Madison, everywhere that you will go
He'll go with you, this is something you should know,
Every step that you take, God will take a look.
Every day of your life has been written in his book.

You are made by him so wonderfully,
You are handpicked for this family,
You are welcomed here so happily,
You are made by him so lovely.
Yes you are.

Madison, you are a gift from above
Made from miracles and love.
Sugar and spice is what you are made of,
Surrounded by our love.

DANIEL'S BLESSING

May God bless you with faith
That is strong, steadfast, and bold.
May he bless you with the blessings
Of the Daniel of old.

May God give you wisdom
Beyond all your years.
May your knowledge and understanding
Be ten times your peers.

May tact and good judgment
Be yours in all things.
May you find favor with men
And the admiration of kings.

May your faith be courageous
As the strong men of Zion.
May God protect you
From the den of the lion.

May the Spirit of the Lord
Dwell richly in you.
May you seek his guidance
In all that you do.

May you seek to be righteous,
May you seek to know truth.
May you know Jesus as Savior
From the days of your youth.

May you talk with God daily,
May he touch your heart anew.
May you worship him only.
He has great plans for you!

May you walk with the Lord
And follow his ways.
May he bless you and keep you
All of your days.

TIANA'S BLESSING

Tiana means "princess" in Greek I am told.
May your life be blessed as Queen Esther of old.

May you grow to be beautiful, strong, and lionhearted.
May you finish well what the Lord has started.

May you be known for your graciousness and charm.
May God protect your loved ones and keep you from harm.

May God keep you in his kind and loving hands,
Whether you are here or in far-off lands.

May God reign in your life, may you know him well.
May your faith be so strong that others can tell

That Jesus is Lord and dwells in your heart,
That his Spirit lives in you and will never depart,

That you are clothed with strength and dignity,
That your life is marked by love and charity,

That you lead with wisdom—it cannot be missed—
That God may use you for such a time as this.

JORDAN'S BLESSING

May you keep strong the faith and keep bright the flame.
May you be mighty as the river that shares your name.

May your faith be as deep as the waters that flow.
May God pour down his blessings from heaven to you below.

As the roots of the mighty oak grow deep by the river,
May your roots of faith grow deep, may you know the Gift and the Giver.

May you be like a cool drink to all whom you know,
A refreshing retreat when the storms of life blow.

As the river gives life and hope to all things,
May you be a well of life from which only goodness springs.

Great blessings upon you may God bestow,
And may the Lord of the Universe be yours to know.

As Jesus came to the river to be baptized by John,
And God's Spirit came upon him as a dove dawned,

May Jesus dwell within you from the days of your youth,
And may his Spirit guide your path in righteousness and truth.

A BLESSING FOR ADDISON
ON THE DAY OF YOUR BAPTISM

Addison, O Little One, you are a daughter of the King,
A royal citizen of heaven, let the angels celebrate and sing.

We are thankful for you and Thomas, we pray with one accord
That your life be blessed as Mary's was, sweet mother of our Lord.

May you grow to be beautiful, strong, and bold.
May your life leave a legacy for generations to behold.

May you be known for your grace, kindness, and charm.
May God protect you and keep you from harm.

May you be clothed with righteousness, strength, and dignity.
May your life be marked by holiness, love, and charity.

May you lead with wisdom, may your mark never miss.
May God use you for such a time as this.

May God reign in your life, may you know him well.
May your faith be so strong that others can tell

That Jesus is Lord and dwells in your heart,
That his Spirit lives in you and cannot depart.

May you know God's voice, and the touch of his hand,
And the breath of his whisper, and his feet in the sand.

May you answer his call, whatever it may be,
May your response be always "Yes, Lord, use me."

May you walk with Jesus, may your journey never end,
May you call him "Lord," and may he call you "Friend."

A BLESSING FOR THOMAS
ON THE DAY OF YOUR BAPTISM

Thomas, your name means "Twin." Double blessings the heavens send,
For God blessed you with Addison, your twin sister and your friend.

May God bless you with faith that is strong, steadfast, and bold.
And may he bless you with the blessings of St. Thomas of old.

May your doubting be small and your faith be brave,
May your life leave a legacy from age to age.

May you believe in things unseen, and hope in things to come,
May your every word and deed reflect the Father and the Son.

May God give you wisdom beyond all your years.
May your knowledge and understanding be above all your peers.

May tact and good judgment be yours in all things.
May you find favor with men and the admiration of kings.

May the Spirit of the Lord dwell richly in you.
May you seek his guidance in all that you do.

May you seek to be righteous, may you seek to know truth.
May you know Jesus as Savior from the days of your youth.

May you talk with God daily, may he touch your heart anew.
May you be still and listen when he whispers to you.

May you walk with the Lord and follow his ways.
May he bless you and call you friend all of your days.

A BLESSING UPON EMMETT
ON THE DAY OF YOUR GRADUATION

Your name means "strength": may you be strong and bold,
May you find your strength in God, as the mighty saints of old.
May your hope be in the Lord, may you rise on eagles' wings.
May you run and not grow weary, may you trust in what God brings.

May your strength be that of Samson, whose strength was from the Lord.
When you are weak may God be strong, and may your faith be restored.
May your courage be that of Joshua, may your valor be contagious.
May it be a source of strength for generations through the ages.

May your heart beat as David's, with humbleness, poetry, and art,
May you know God, and may he call you "A man after my own heart."
May he be your refuge and your strength, may you know no fear.
May you lean on him when trouble comes, may you know he is always near.

May you talk with your Lord daily, may he touch your heart anew,
May your heart be still and listen, when he whispers to you.
May you know God's Spirit is with you, wherever you may go.
The highest hills, the deepest seas, even there, he knows your soul.

May wisdom, peace, and joy be yours, I ask the Lord these things.
May he grant you faith and hope and love and shelter under his wings.
May he guide your path and lead you home, may his light lead your way.
May you call him "Lord" and may he call you "Friend," now and all of your days.

A BLESSING UPON ANNE
ON YOUR BAT MITZVAH

Today you start a journey, may your journey never end.
May you always grow in the Lord, Jehovah Elohim.
From the House of Israel, from where Abraham has trod,
May you grow to be a Noble Woman of God.

Your name means "Grace," may you be Brave and Bold,
May your Life be filled with Grace as God's Great Women of Old:
Sarah, Esther, Deborah, Ruth—
Great Women of Faith, Humble Women of Truth.

May your Faith be as Sarah's—Fearless and Strong,
May you walk in His promises all your life long.
May you always be Thankful, may you give the Lord your best,
May you be forever Joyful, may you be forever Blessed.

May you be clothed as Ruth, with Strength and Dignity.
May your Life be marked by Righteousness, Goodness, and Charity.
May you be known for Graciousness, Kindness, and Love.
May God's own hand Protect you when you seek Refuge from Above.

May you lead with Wisdom, may your mark never miss.
Like Esther, may God use you for such a Time as this.
May you answer his call, whatever it may be,
May your response be as Deborah's—"Yes, Lord, use me."

May El Shaddai reign in your Heart, may you know him well,
May your Faith be so Strong that others can tell
That the Word of the Lord is written on your Heart,
That his Spirit lives within you and cannot depart.

May you know God's voice and the touch of his Hand
And the breath of his Whisper and his Footprints on the sand.
May you walk with Yahweh, may your journey never end.
May you always call him "Lord," and may he ever call you "Friend."

You are called to the Torah; you are called to the God of Abraham.
May you know the One who has called you; may you know the Great I Am.

BLESSINGS OF GIRLFRIENDS: WRITING YOUR OWN BLESSINGS

꧁

Since graduation from Augustana College in 1985, I have celebrated the ups and cried through the downs of life with a core group of girlfriends. Each one of us is so different, and I love the uniqueness we each bring to our friendship. One of our traditions which we never miss is an annual Christmas gathering where we exchange gifts. We each pick a number from a hat, and when our number is up, we can either pick one gift from the pile of unopened gifts or steal an opened gift from another person who has already chosen one. It's always best to have the highest number so that one has the most options to choose from!

For our twenty-fifth annual Christmas exchange, I made framed blessings for each of my girlfriends to remind them of how much I appreciated having them in my life. I researched the meaning of each of their names, and unsurprisingly, found that the meanings matched their personalities! I also wove in a number of words that described each woman's spirit, her history, and the lovely things that came to mind when I thought of her. And finally, I included a prayer of thanks to God for making each one of them so wondrously and wonderfully. I printed the blessings in an Old English font on parchment, mounted them on beautiful Florentine paper, and put them in lovely 8x10 antique gold frames. What a hit! I have included the blessings here.

If you, gentle reader, would like to carry on the timeless custom of giving a blessing to special people who have been blessings to you, this simple formula is a great way to start your own tradition of showing how much you appreciate friends and loved ones.

LISA

Hebrew: "God is my oath." Tall, beauty, intelligent, doctor, introspective, challenging, sensitive, family, positive, calm, unflustered, caring, open, thoughtful, classic, spiritual, reflective, God-centered, supportive, Waukegan, Augustana, Chicago, Wisconsin, daughter, sister, wife, mother, friend, blessing

. . .

Lord, I will praise you because you alone created Lisa's inner being. You knit her together inside her mother. I give you thanks because Lisa has been so amazingly and miraculously made. Your work in making Lisa is wonderful.
—Psalm 139:13–14

KELLY

Celtic: "Bright headed." Beauty, gracious, porcelain, elegant, mischievous, creative, poised, laughter, fun, design, naughty, Fox River Grove, Augustana, daughter, sister, wife, mother, friend, blessing . . .

Lord, I will praise you because you alone created Kelly's inner being. You knit her together inside her mother. I give you thanks because Kelly has been so amazingly and miraculously made. Your work in making Kelly is wonderful.
—Psalm 139:13–14

ELIZABETH

Hebrew: "God is my oath." Sensitive, caring, giving, thoughtful, classic, elegant, righteous, heartfelt, soulful, spiritual, reflective, Christ-centered, supportive, Arlington Heights, Augustana, Crystal Lake, daughter, sister, twin, wife, mother, friend, blessing . . .

Lord, I will praise you because you alone created Elizabeth's inner being. You knit her together inside her mother. I give you thanks because Elizabeth has been so amazingly and miraculously made. Your work in making Elizabeth is wonderful.
—Psalm 139: 13–14

MIRIAM

Hebrew: "Wished-for child; rebellious; strong waters." Strong, brave, courageous, caring, leader, teacher, laughter, rebellious, classic, wisdom, righteous, truthful, intelligent, spiritual, athlete, confident, Christ-centered, supportive, Metamora, Augustana, Mount Prospect, daughter, sister, twin, wife, mother, friend, blessing . . .

Lord, I will praise you because you alone created Miriam's inner being. You knit her together inside her mother. I give you thanks because Miriam has been so amazingly and miraculously made. Your work in making Miriam is wonderful.
—Psalm 139:13–14

A BLESSING UPON CYNTHIA
ON THE DAY OF YOUR FIFTIETH BIRTHDAY

Your name means "Goddess of the Moon",
May you always reflect the Son.
May your Light so shine before others
That you are known by the Works you have done.

May you always be Beautiful,
May you be Wise and Brave.
May your Life's Work be an Inheritance
For generations, from age to age.

May you lead with Righteousness,
May Kindness and Charity never miss,
May you be clothed in Strength.
May God use you for such as time as this.

May the Spirit of God
Dwell richly in you.
May you seek the Lord's Guidance
In all that you say and do.

May God use you as his Vessel,
May your Soul be his Dwelling Place.
May your Life be his Canvas
Upon which he paints his Amazing Grace.

May your Family rise to bless you,
May they walk where you have trod.
May they call you "My Mother—the Gracious One;
My Wife—A Woman of God."

May you talk with your Lord daily
And may he touch your Heart anew.
May your soul be still and listen
When he whispers to you.

May you always walk with Jesus,
May your Journey never end.
May you forever call him "Lord,"
And may he always call you "Friend."

FINAL WORDS OF BLESSING

❧

Dear Friends,

Our words can give life. Our words can tell others that we believe in them even more than they believe in themselves. Our words can be the magic dust that, when sprinkled on another, can spur them on to great things. Our words can be those that inspire, bless, and encourage. Our calling as followers of Christ is to be Jesus with skin on. The only hands and feet God has here on earth are ours. The only eyes and ears God has here on earth are ours. The only mouth God has here on earth is ours. Let our words be blessings, prayers, and gifts of grace.

The prophet Micah asked the question, "What does the Lord require of you?" The Lord answered: "To act justly, and to love mercy, and to walk humbly with your God" (Micah 6:8). And so, gentle reader, I leave you with this blessing of a lifelong, humble walk with your God:

May you talk with your Lord daily
And may he touch your Heart anew.
May your soul be still and listen
When he whispers to you.

May you always walk with Jesus,
May your Journey never end.
May you forever call him "Lord,"
And may he always call you "Friend."

THE BLESSING COLLECTION AND CONTACT INFORMATION

What started as a gift to dear friends on the day of their wedding has blossomed. Babies came, and then new houses, and then other meaningful celebrations for which I gave framed blessings, each covered with a prayer that my words would be God's words and that the Holy Spirit would use God's words, openly displayed in homes, to bless and inspire. Friends started requesting certain blessings: "Do you have a blessing for a friend of mine whose father has died?" "Do you have a fireman's blessing?" "My daughter is getting married. Do you have a bride's blessing?" "My son is graduating. Can you write a blessing for him?" Over the course of the years, the Spirit has led me to write a number of blessings for loved ones and friends. Then the pivotal question came: "Do you have a website?"

From these humble beginnings, the prodding of loved ones, and the nudging of the Holy Spirit, a fledgling company emerged: The Blessing Collection by Inspiration Breaks. Not surprisingly, our tagline is *Words of Inspiration, Blessing, and Encouragement.*™ On our website, www.theblessingscollection.com and www.blessingsframed.com, and in select retail stores, we offer high-quality, beautiful, and elegant framed blessings and greeting cards that celebrate the special occasions and special people in our lives with meaningful, Spirit-filled gifts. Each blessing can be personalized with the name of the recipient for a unique heirloom gift that will be cherished for years to come. Our magnificent frames are made in the USA, and many of our gorgeous papers and tapestries are imported from Italy. New blessings are created on a regular basis as the Holy Spirit moves and as requested by friends and customers.

Friends of The Blessing Collection can sign up for a free inspirational devotional designed to inspire, bless, and encourage each of us as we go about our busy lives. The devotional, dubbed *Inspiration Breaks,* is sent about twice a month via e-mail. It also gets posted as a blog on the website. To request *Inspiration Breaks* to be sent to your e-mail, just drop me an e-mail at the address below.

If you enjoyed this book, I invite you to drop me an e-mail, send a postcard, write a review on Amazon, pick up the phone and call, post a comment on my website or the website of The Blessing Collection, or just stop by for coffee and a chat. I would love to get your feedback and thoughts for future blessings, books, and projects that bring Words of Inspiration, Blessing, and Encouragement.™

Please send correspondence to:

Charlene Quint Kalebic
Inspiration Breaks LLC
PO Box 230 / 230 Northgate
Lake Forest, IL 60045
(o) 847-505-8069
E-mail me at charlene@blessingsframed.com or info@blessingsframed.com.
You can also find me on the following websites:
www.charlenequintkalebic.com
or
www.theblessingscollection.com
or
www.blessingsframed.com